AF454157

מסילת ישרים

The Way to Spiritual Integrity

Unifying Spirit and Action

Ramchal
Rabbi Moshe Chaim Luzzatto

Translated by
Rav Raphael Afilalo

Hazohar555@gmail.com

kabbalah5.com - zoharvideos.com – ramchal.com

YouTube: Rav Raphael Afilalo – Zohar - Kabbalah

ISBN: 978-2-925501-01-5

Dépôt légal, Bibliothèque et Archives nationales du Québec, 2024

Copyright © 2024 – Raphael Afilalo

All rights reserved to Raphael Afilalo. No part of this book may be reproduced or transmitted in any form without the written permission of the author. Except for the inclusion of brief quotations in a review.

Publications by Rav Raphael Afilalo

English	French
Concepts of Kabbalah	Concepts de Kabbalah
Kabbalah Dictionary	Dictionnaire de Kabbalah
Glossary of Kabbalah	Glossaire de Kabbalah
Arizal Prince of the Kabbalists	Arizal Prince des Kabbalistes
160 Questions on the Kabbalah	160 Questions sur la Kabbalah
Kabbalah of the Arizal, according to the Ramchal	Kabbalah du Arizal, selon le Ramhal
Gates of Reincarnations	Portes des Réincarnations

Translations of books of the Ramchal by R. Raphael Afilalo

God and His Ways	Dieu et Ses Voies
The Kabbalist and the Philosopher	Le Kabbaliste et le Philosophe
The Way to spiritual integrity	La voie vers l'intégrité spirituelle
The Wisdom of Consciousness	La Sagesse de la Conscience

בעברית

מושגי חכמת הקבלה

חשיבות לימוד הזהר

אריז''ל נשיא המקובלים

קיצור כתבי האר

קבלה – תורה האמת

הזהר – כתבים מיסטיים של פנמיוה התורה

The life of the Ramchal

Moshe Chaim Luzzatto, known as the Ramchal, was an enigmatic figure in Jewish history, remembered as a philosopher, kabbalist, and poet whose works have had a lasting impact on Jewish thought and mysticism. Born in Padua, Italy, on April 26, 1707, into a distinguished family, Ramchal displayed prodigious intellectual capabilities from a young age.

His education was comprehensive, steeped in the dual worlds of Jewish and secular knowledge, which was a hallmark of the Italian Jewish renaissance. He was well-versed in the Torah, Talmud, and Kabbalistic literature, as well as the sciences and philosophy of his time, which informed his unique approach to Jewish theology and ethics.

The Ramchal's intellectual journey began with his study of the Talmud and other classic Jewish texts, but he was particularly drawn to the study of Kabbalah, the Jewish mystical tradition. By the age of 20, he had already begun writing his own commentaries on these subjects. His most famous work, "Mesillat Yesharim" (Path of the Just), is a systematic exploration of Jewish ethics and spiritual growth, which has become a foundational text in the Mussar movement, a Jewish ethical, educational, and cultural movement.

Despite his young age, the Ramchal's works, such as "Derech Hashem" (God and His Ways), which systematically presents the fundamentals of Jewish belief, demonstrated a mastery of Jewish law and mysticism that few could rival. He also penned "Da'at Tevunot" (The Knowing Heart), a dialogue between the intellect and the soul on the nature of God's interaction with the world, and the purpose of Creation and human existence.

However, the Ramchal's intense involvement with Kabbalah, at a time when skepticism towards mysticism was widespread following the false messianic movement of Shabbetai Zvi, aroused suspicion. His formation of a select group of disciples to study Kabbalah led to further controversy. In 1727, under communal pressure in Italy, he agreed to a ban on teaching Kabbalah and ceased writing Kabbalistic works. This period of conflict was difficult for the Ramchal, whose only desire was to elevate the spiritual state of his people.

In search of a more accommodating environment for his Kabbalistic pursuits, Ramchal left Italy in 1735, eventually settling in Amsterdam. There, he hoped to live a life of spiritual and intellectual freedom. He supported himself by working as a diamond cutter and continued to write extensively. Amsterdam's Jewish community was a center of publishing, and it was there that he printed many of his works.

The Ramchal's life in Amsterdam allowed him some respite from the controversies that had followed him in Italy, and he continued his prolific writing, including works on Hebrew grammar and logic, such as "Sefer haHigayon" (The Book of Logic), which reflected his broader academic interests.

The Way to Spiritual Integrity

Despite his relatively comfortable life in Amsterdam, the Ramchal's longing for the Land of Israel was intense. In 1743, he and his family made the arduous journey to the Holy Land, settling in Acre. Tragically, his time there was short-lived; he died in a plague along with his family in 1746, at the young age of 39.

The Ramchal left behind a literary legacy that spans philosophical treatises, ethical texts, kabbalistic writings, poetry, plays, and more. His works continue to be studied for their depth and insight into the human condition and the divine.

Perhaps the most enduring aspect of the Ramchal's work is his ability to synthesize the mystical and rational aspects of Judaism. He believed that an understanding of the divine structure of the universe could lead to a profound religious life rooted in ethical conduct. His works have been embraced by various streams of Jewish thought, from the rationalist to the mystic, each finding in his writings a wellspring of knowledge and inspiration.

The legacy of the Ramchal is marked by a balance between the esoteric and the practical, the heavenly and the earthly. His vision of spiritual ascent is not one of withdrawal from the world but of engagement with it, guided by divine wisdom. His life and works serve as a bridge, inviting each person to traverse the gap between the finite and infinite, between human and divine potential.

The *Maggid* of Mezritch said:
"His generation did not merit this great man.... Many among our people, through lack of knowledge, have uttered on this saintly man calumny that was not justified."

The Gaon of Vilna declared that if Ramchal was still alive, he would have traveled to Italy on foot to learn from his wisdom.

Moshe Chaim Luzzatto's contributions to Jewish thought and his teachings are now universally recognized as treasures of Jewish literature, offering guidance to those who seek a path of righteousness, intellect, and spiritual introspection. The Ramchal remains a beacon of spiritual and moral guidance, whose influence continues to be felt centuries after his passing.

Forward

The Way to Spiritual Integrity (Mesilat Yesharim) by the Ramchal, Rabbi Moshe Chaim Luzzatto, is a timeless classic of Jewish thought, a luminous guide to ethical and spiritual perfection. Written in the 18th century, this text remains astonishingly relevant, illuminating the path for generations of men and women in search of meaning and elevation. A true manual of personal development according to the Torah, Mesilat Yesharim invites us to an inner journey, a methodical ascent to the highest levels of holiness accessible to the human being.

The Ramchal himself embodies this constant aspiration to perfection. Born in 1707 in Padua, Italy, he distinguished himself from a young age by the breadth of his knowledge and his spiritual depth. Versed in all fields of Jewish knowledge - Tanakh, Talmud, Halakha, Kabbalah, Mussar - as well as in the sciences and philosophy of his time, he developed a unique approach to spiritual life, based on a harmonious synthesis between reason and mysticism, study and interiority, intellectual rigor and fervor. His journey was marked by misunderstanding and controversy, leading him from Italy to Amsterdam and then to the Land of Israel, where he passed away at the age of 39, leaving behind a work of astounding richness and originality.

It is in this context that the writing of Mesilat Yesharim in 1738 took place. Far from being an abstract theoretical treatise, the work is eminently practical, rooted in the lived experience of man in this world. Its starting point is simple and clear: the purpose of human existence is to delight in attachment to God, and this is what we must strive for with all our might. But the way is long and strewn with obstacles, requiring method and discernment. The Ramchal then takes us by the hand and guides us step by step on the spiritual rungs leading to holiness.

The very structure of the book reflects this progression. The Ramchal defines a series of attributes or ethical levels to be cultivated in a specific order, each being a prerequisite for the next: caution (zehirut), diligence (zerizut), cleanliness (nekiyut), abstinence (perishut), purity (tahara), piety (hassidut), humility (anavah), fear of sin (yir'at het), and holiness (kedushah). He dedicates one or more chapters to each of these attributes, explaining their nature, components, means of acquisition, and obstacles. Each theme is illustrated by numerous rabbinical sources that give it depth and legitimacy. Far from being a mechanical sequence of states to traverse, these attributes form a coherent whole, a life itinerary leading to the fulfillment of our vocation as beings created in the image of God.

At the heart of this teaching lies the notion of responsibility. For the Ramchal, man is a being of choice and consciousness, invested with a divine mission. Each of our actions, words, or thoughts has an impact that surpasses us. Far from being insignificant, our daily acts contribute to the sanctification or desecration of the Divine Name. Hence the importance of vigilance (zehirut), the first milestone on the path of the just, which enjoins us to constantly examine our ways in light of our duty as human beings, to avoid evil and do good.

But this demand for perfection is not meant to crush us. On the contrary, it reveals our greatness by calling us to collaborate in the divine project. The Ramchal repeatedly emphasizes the infinite goodness of the Creator and His desire to bestow true goodness upon us. The mitzvot are not a burden but an invaluable gift, an opportunity to embrace the divine will and find meaning and fulfillment. Every effort on our part, however small, elicits an immeasurable flow of blessings in return. It is with love and joy that we must embrace our vocation, in the dazzled awareness of serving the Master of the universe.

This fertile tension between responsibility and trust permeates all of Mesilat Yesharim. Man appears in his fragility and greatness, his smallness before infinity, and his unlimited potential for elevation. The Ramchal urges us to an uncompromising lucidity regarding our failings while encouraging us to persevere relentlessly in the pursuit of good. He warns us against the pitfalls of pride, anger, or jealousy and guides us toward humility, serenity, and selfless love. His teaching is neither moralistic nor ascetic: he invites us to enjoy the delights of holiness, to find the most intense happiness in closeness to our Creator.

Beyond its actual content, it is the beauty of its language and the power of its images that leave a lasting impression on us. The Ramchal 's style combines conceptual rigor and poetic sensitivity, subtle analysis of soul movements, and evocative power of metaphors. The parables illuminating his discourse will remain engraved in the reader's mind for a long time, such as the one about the man lost in a labyrinth who manages to reach the center and can guide his companions, or the son striving to anticipate the desires of his beloved father. The Ramchal excels in finely depicting inner states, struggles, and aspirations that inhabit us. As a master of wisdom, he knows how to find the words that awaken, challenge, and elevate.

Mesilat Yesharim has thus become, over the generations, a precious companion for countless seekers of truth. Studied assiduously in yeshivot as well as by laypeople, it is an inexhaustible source of inspiration and guidance. Its influence has far transcended the Jewish world to deeply touch all those who aspire to a life of meaning and righteousness. More than two centuries after its writing, it has lost none of its force and relevance, for it addresses the most essential and urgent questions of the human condition.

In a world lacking bearings, bewildered by the pursuit of material success and the glorification of the ego, the Ramchal 's voice resounds like a saving call to return to the essential, to realign our existence with eternal values. His vision of man as a being of mission and self-transcendence is a breath of fresh air, an antidote to ambient depression and nihilism. Rooting us in the tradition of our Sages while opening infinite horizons, Mesilat Yesharim rekindles our thirst for greatness, purity, and fullness. It offers us an Ariadne's thread to traverse the maze of life and access, step by step, true joy, that of closeness to our Creator.

Studying Mesilat Yesharim means engaging in an exhilarating process of inner transformation. It means sharpening one's ethical discernment, strengthening one's will, and refining one's sensitivity. It means learning to see the hand of Providence in every corner of our existence, to make our daily lives an offering of holiness. There is no need for extraordinary feats or extreme renunciations: it is enough to humbly, conscientiously advance on our own path, cultivating the virtues that will make us sincere and joyful servants.

May the study of this wonderful work kindle in us the spark of burning desire to draw closer to our beloved Father and enjoy the sweetness of His presence at every moment of our lives. May we, by meditating on the inspired words of the Ramchal, find the courage and determination to lead a righteous and holy life and thus contribute to the repair of the world under divine sovereignty. This is the wish expressed by the Ramchal himself in the preamble to his book, calling upon the reader the blessing of the Most High: "May the Eternal be our support, keep our feet from stumbling, and may the prayer of the beloved psalmist be fulfilled in us: 'Teach me Your way, so that I may walk in Your truth; unite my heart to fear Your Name.' Amen, may it be His will."

Introduction by Rabbi Moshe Chaim Luzzatto

The author said: I did not compose this work to teach people what they do not know, but to remind them of what is already known and widely publicized among them. For you will not find in most of my words anything but matters that most people know and do not doubt at all. However, just as these matters are widely known and their truth is clear to all, forgetfulness of them is also very common and prevalent. Therefore, the benefit derived from this book does not come from reading it once, for it is possible that the reader will not find novel ideas in his mind after reading it that were not there before reading it, except a little. Rather, the benefit comes from reviewing it and persevering with it, for these matters that are naturally forgotten by people will be remembered, and one will take to heart one's duty which one overlooks.

If you consider the current state of most of the world, you will see that most people of quick understanding and sharp intellect apply most of their analysis and contemplation to the intricacies of different wisdoms and the depth of theoretical studies, each person according to his intellectual inclination and natural desire. Some exert great effort in studying the creation and nature, while others devote all of their theoretical analysis to astronomy and geometry, and others to crafts. Yet others delve further into the holy, that is, the study of the sacred Torah some in the give and take of halachic discussions, some in midrashim, and some in halachic rulings. But few belong to the category that establishes the study and analysis of matters of perfection in divine service, of love, fear, attachment, and all the other aspects of piety (chassidut).

This is not because these matters are not fundamental principles to them, for if you ask them, each one will say that this is the main principle. One cannot imagine a truly wise person for whom all these matters are not clear. Rather, the reason that they do not apply much analysis to it is due to the matters being so well-known and simple to them that they do not see a need to spend much time analyzing them. The study of these matters and the reading of books of this type is left only to those whose intellect is not so sharp and close to being coarse. You will see them diligent in all this and not budging from it, to the point that according to the practice prevalent in the world, when you see a pious individual, you cannot avoid suspecting him of being of coarse intellect.

However, the results of this practice are very detrimental for both the wise and the unwise, for it causes both to lack true piety, making it very rare to find in the world. It is lacking in the wise due to their limited analysis of it, and lacking in the unwise due to their limited grasp of it. As a result, most people imagine that piety depends on reciting many psalms, very long confessions, difficult fasts, and immersions in ice and snow all matters with which the intellect is not content and the mind is not at ease.

True piety, which is desirable and pleasant, is far from our conceptual image. It is a simple matter that which is not a person's obligation, he does not have in mind. Even though its basic principles are already fixed in the heart of every upright person, if he does not engage in them, he will see their details without recognizing them; he will encounter them without noticing them. See that matters of piety and matters of fear and love and purity of heart are not matters ingrained in a person such that he does not need means to acquire them. People do not find them on their own just as they find all of their natural functions like sleep and wakefulness, hunger and satiety, and all the other functions engraved in our nature. Rather, they certainly require means and strategies to acquire them, and there are also factors that detract from them and distance them from a person. There is no lack of ways to distance their detriments. If so, how can one not need to spend time analyzing this matter in order to know the truth of these matters, to know the way to acquire them and uphold them? From where will this wisdom come into a person's heart if he does not seek it?

Once the need for perfection in divine service and the obligation of its purity and cleanliness has been affirmed by every wise person for without these it is certainly not desired at all, but despised and abhorred, as "the L-rd searches all hearts and understands the inclination of all thoughts" (Chronicles 1:29:17) how will we respond on the day of rebuke if we were negligent in this analysis and abandoned a matter that is so incumbent upon us, as it is the essence of what the L-rd our G-d asks of us? Is it conceivable that our intellect would toil and labor in analyses that we are not obligated in, in give-and-takes from which we derive no benefit, and in laws that do not apply to us, while we leave the great duty that we owe to our Creator to habit and treat it as rote learned from others? If we did not contemplate and analyze what is true fear and its branches, how will we acquire it and how will we escape from the worldly vanity that causes us to forget it?

Will it not be forgotten and lost even though we know it is our duty? Love, likewise if we do not strive to instill it in our hearts with the force of all the means that bring us to it, how will we find it within us? From where will attachment and passion for Him, may He be blessed, and His Torah come into our souls if we do not pay heed to His greatness and His exaltedness, which give birth to this attachment in our hearts? How will our thoughts be purified if we do not strive to cleanse them of the blemishes that the physical nature inflicts upon them, along with all of the character traits that likewise require correction and straightening who will straighten them and who will correct them if we do not pay attention to them and do not examine the matter with great precision? Indeed, if we would analyze the matter with true analysis, we would find it in its true form and benefit ourselves, and we would teach it to others and benefit them as well.

This is as Solomon said: "If you seek it like silver and search for it as for treasures, then you will understand the fear of the L-rd" (Proverbs 2:4-5). He does not say, "Then you will understand philosophy, then you will understand astronomy, then you will understand medicine, then you will understand laws, then you will understand halachot," but rather, "Then you will understand the fear of the L-rd." You see that in order to understand fear, you must seek it like silver and search for it like treasures. Indeed, in what we have been taught by our forefathers and in what is well-known to every intelligent person in general terms will time be found for all other areas of analysis but not for this analysis? Why should a person not set aside times, at the very least, for this contemplation, if he is compelled to turn to other analyses or pursuits in the rest of his time?

The verse states, "Behold, the fear of the Lord is wisdom" (Job 28:28), and our Sages, may their memory be for a blessing, said (Shabbat 31b): "'Behold' means one, as in Greek they call 'one' hen." We see that fear is wisdom, and it alone is wisdom. Certainly, that which does not involve analysis is not called wisdom. But the truth is that great analysis is needed for all these matters to know them truthfully and not by imagination and false reasoning, and all the more so to acquire them and attain them.

One who contemplates them will see that piety does not depend on those matters that the foolish pietists imagine, but on matters of true perfection and great wisdom. This is what Moses our teacher, peace be upon him, teaches us when he says: "And now, Israel, what does the Lord your G-d ask of you, but to fear the Lord your G-d, to walk in all His ways, and to love Him, and to serve the Lord your G-d with all your heart and with all your soul, to keep the commandments of the Lord and His statutes?" (Deuteronomy 10:12). Here he encapsulated all the elements of the perfection of the service that is desirable to His blessed Name, which are: fear, walking in His ways, love, wholeness of heart, and observing all the commandments.

Fear is the awe of His exaltedness, may He be blessed, such that one fears Him as one would fear a great and awesome king, and is embarrassed before His greatness with regard to every movement that one is about to make, and certainly when speaking before Him in prayer or engaging in His Torah. Walking in His ways includes the entire matter of the rectitude of one's character traits and their correction, and this is what they, may their memory be for a blessing, explained: "Just as He is merciful, so should you be merciful" (Shabbat 133b), and the general principle of all this is that a person should conduct all of his character traits and all types of his actions according to integrity and morality.

Our Sages, may their memory be for a blessing, encapsulated it as "All that brings glory to its Maker and glory to him from man" (Avot 2:1), meaning all that leads to the ultimate true good, meaning that its outcome is the reinforcement of the Torah and the betterment of the fellowship of states. Love is that love for Him, may He be blessed, should be instilled in a person's heart to the point that his soul is aroused to do what is pleasing before Him, just as one's heart is aroused to do what is pleasing to his father and mother, and he is distressed if this is lacking on his part or on the part of others, and he is zealous for this and rejoices greatly when he does something of this.

Wholeness of heart means that the service before Him, may He be blessed, should be with purity of intent, meaning for the sole purpose of serving Him and not for any other motive. Included in this is that one should be whole in service and not like one who hobbles between two opinions or like one who performs the commandments by rote, but that one's entire heart should be devoted to this. Observing all the commandments: As its literal meaning, that is, observing all the commandments with all their details and conditions.

Now, all these are general principles that require great explanation. I found that our Sages, may their memory be for a blessing, summarized these parts in a different order, more detailed and arranged according to the necessary progression in acquiring them properly. This is what they said in a baraita, cited in various places in the Talmud, one of them in the chapter "Before Their Festivals." These are their words: "From here Rabbi Pinchas ben Yair said: Torah leads to vigilance, vigilance leads to zeal, zeal leads to cleanliness, cleanliness leads to separation, separation leads to purity, purity leads to piety, piety leads to humility, humility leads to fear of sin, fear of sin leads to holiness, holiness leads to Divine inspiration, Divine inspiration leads to the resurrection of the dead."

Based on this baraita, I decided to compose this work to teach myself and remind others of the conditions for perfect service, according to their levels. I will explain regarding each one its matters and parts or details, the way to acquire it and what detracts from it, and the way to be vigilant against them. For I will read it, and so will all who find contentment in it, so that we may learn to fear the L-rd our G-d, and our duty before Him will not be forgotten by us. And that which the corporeality of nature strives to remove from our heart, the reading and contemplation will bring to our memory and arouse us to what we are commanded. May the L-rd be our support and guard our feet from being trapped, and may the request of the psalmist, beloved to his G-d, be fulfilled in us: "Teach me Your way, O Lord, that I may walk in Your truth; unite my heart to fear Your Name" (Psalms 86:11). Amen, may this be His will.

Summaries of each chapter

Introduction

In the introduction, Rabbi Moshe Chaim Luzzatto (Ramchal) explains his purpose in writing this book. He emphasizes that he is not teaching new concepts but reminding readers of well-known truths that are often forgotten. The goal is to internalize these truths through repeated study and reflection. Ramchal warns against the distractions and forgetfulness that can cause even the most fundamental principles to be neglected. He urges readers to engage continuously in the pursuit of spiritual perfection and the true understanding of divine service.

Chapter 1 - Man's duty in the world

This chapter explains that man was created to delight in god in the world to come, and that this world is a means to reach that end. mitzvot are presented as the means to achieve this ultimate goal. attachment to god is described as true perfection. the author emphasizes that man is placed in a world full of temptations and trials, and if he triumphs, he merits attachment to god.

Chapter 2 - Vigilance

This chapter defines vigilance as paying attention to one's actions. the author presents this as an obligation dictated by reason, while recognizing that the evil inclination seeks to prevent this reflection. it encourages overcoming this obstacle and constantly examining one's ways, emphasizing that this requires strength and insight.

Chapter 3 - Levels of vigilance

This chapter details the different levels of vigilance. it begins by emphasizing the importance of understanding the true good to choose and the true evil to flee. the author insists on the need to examine one's actions at the time of doing them and afterwards, to weigh each gesture before doing it, and to review and analyze all past actions.

Chapter 4 - Acquiring vigilance

This chapter explores ways to acquire vigilance. the author emphasizes that torah study leads to vigilance. he stresses the importance of contemplating the gravity of divine service and judgment. the text presents different levels of reflection for different people: for the most elevated, it's the search for perfection; for the intermediates, it's the fear of future judgment; and for the masses, it's consideration of the needs of this world.

Chapter 5 - Destructive causes of vigilance

This chapter identifies three main destroyers of vigilance: worldly preoccupations, mockery, and bad company. the author explains how worldly preoccupations prevent reflection on one's actions, how mockery makes one insensitive to reproaches and moral awakening, and how bad company leads to neglecting one's duty out of conformism.

Chapter 6 - Zeal

This chapter deals with zeal, presented as the logical continuation of vigilance. the author explains that zeal concerns the fulfillment of positive commandments, while vigilance relates to negative commandments. he emphasizes the importance of quickly seizing opportunities to perform mitzvot and carrying them out with eagerness.

Chapter 7 - Degrees of zeal

This chapter explores the different degrees of zeal. the author distinguishes two aspects: zeal before action and zeal during action. he explains the importance of hurrying to seize an opportunity for a mitzvah and completing it quickly once started. the text cites biblical and talmudic examples to illustrate the importance of zeal.

Chapter 8 - Acquiring zeal

This chapter discusses ways to acquire zeal. the author explains that the methods are similar to those used to acquire vigilance. he emphasizes the importance of meditating on the value of mitzvot and on the numerous favors that god constantly grants. the text encourages realizing that all our well-being depends on god, which should naturally push us to serve him zealously.

Chapter 9 - Hindrances to zeal

This chapter identifies the main obstacles to zeal. the author cites the search for physical comfort, excessive fear of difficulties, and the habit of laziness as the main hindrances. he encourages adopting the attitude of a worker or soldier, always ready for action. the text warns against excuses and justifications that one can give to avoid effort.

Chapter 10 - Cleanliness

This chapter deals with spiritual cleanliness. the author defines it as the state of being completely cleansed of any bad trait and any sin. he explains the difference between vigilance and cleanliness, the latter being a higher level where even subtle temptations are eliminated. the text emphasizes the difficulty of reaching this level, but encourages aspiring to it.

Chapter 11 - Aspects of cleanliness

This chapter explores in detail the different aspects of spiritual cleanliness. the author addresses topics such as honesty in business, purity in interpersonal relationships, mastery of speech, and control of thoughts. he emphasizes the importance of being vigilant even in areas where the law seems permissive. the text also deals with character traits to be purified, such as pride, anger, jealousy and covetousness.

Chapter 12 - Acquiring cleanliness

This last chapter presents ways to acquire spiritual cleanliness. the author emphasizes the importance of constant study of sacred texts and ethical works. he explains that this study allows one to know the nuances of mitzvot and character traits, and to remain vigilant in their application. the text encourages regular reading to counter natural forgetfulness and stimulate new reflections.

Chapter 13 - Abstinence

This chapter explains that abstinence is the beginning of holiness. it distinguishes three levels: the prohibitions themselves, rabbinical decrees, and personal restrictions. proper abstinence consists of taking from the world only what is absolutely necessary, in order to avoid the traps of sin. however, one must find a balance and not abstain from necessary things.

Chapter 14 - Aspects of abstinence

This chapter details the three main aspects of abstinence: in pleasures, in laws, and in customs. abstinence in pleasures consists of limiting worldly pleasures. abstinence in laws involves being strict even in doubtful cases. abstinence in customs consists of partially withdrawing from society to focus on divine service.

Chapter 15 - Acquiring abstinence

This chapter explains how to acquire abstinence, mainly through contemplation of the inferiority of worldly pleasures. it emphasizes the importance of solitude and gradually moving away from the vanities of the world. it warns against the dangers of associating with people who seek honors and pleasures.

Chapter 16 - Purity

This chapter deals with purity of heart and thoughts. it explains that even necessary physical actions must be performed with pure intention, without seeking pleasure for its own sake. it emphasizes the importance of acting solely to please god, without mixing in other motivations.

Chapter 17 - Acquiring purity

This chapter explores ways to acquire purity. it emphasizes the importance of deep reflection on the inferiority of worldly pleasures and contemplation of divine greatness. it recommends mental preparation before performing religious acts and warns against worldly concerns that can distract from purity of intention.

Chapter 18 - Piety

This chapter defines piety as the expansion of fulfilling commandments beyond the strict minimum required. it explains that true piety requires deep understanding and can only be achieved by those who have already acquired other spiritual qualities. piety involves seeking to do what pleases god, even beyond what is explicitly commanded.

Chapter 19 - Parts of piety

This chapter details the three main aspects of piety: the act, the manner of doing, and the intention. it explains how piety applies in relationships between man and god, as well as between men. it emphasizes the importance of benevolence, honor given to others, and attention to details in fulfilling commandments.

Chapter 20 - Ladder of piety

This chapter presents piety as a difficult ladder to climb, requiring three elements: pure intention, careful analysis of one's actions, and trust in god. it warns against the dangers of misjudging pious actions and emphasizes the importance of considering the consequences of each act.

Chapter 21 - Acquiring piety

This chapter explores ways to acquire piety. it emphasizes the importance of introspection and contemplation of divine greatness and his goodness towards us. it recommends reading psalms and studying the acts of the pious. it warns against obstacles such as worldly concerns and pleasures, and emphasizes the importance of trust in god.

Chapter 22 - Humility

This chapter defines humility as not considering oneself important for any reason. it explains that humility must first be in thought, then in action. it emphasizes that even positive qualities should not be a source of pride, but rather of gratitude towards god. it details different aspects of humility, such as tolerance of insults and fleeing from honors.

Chapter 23 - Acquiring humility

This chapter discusses ways to acquire humility. it recommends practicing modest behaviors and contemplating our natural lowliness. it warns against the dangers of flattery and emphasizes the importance of seeking honest friends who will help us see our faults.

Chapter 24 - Fear of sin

This chapter distinguishes different types of fear: fear of punishment, fear of divine greatness, and fear of sin. it explains that fear of sin is a constant anxiety about committing a fault, even involuntarily. it emphasizes that this fear is difficult to achieve and requires constant awareness of the divine presence.

Chapter 25 - Acquiring fear

This chapter explains how to acquire fear of sin. it emphasizes the importance of contemplating the divine presence everywhere and his supervision of all things. it stresses the need for constant study and reflection to maintain this awareness.

Chapter 26 - Holiness

This final chapter deals with holiness as the ultimate spiritual level. it explains that holiness begins with human effort but is completed by a divine gift. it describes holiness as a constant attachment to god, where even physical actions become sacred. it emphasizes that this level can only be achieved after acquiring all the other spiritual qualities discussed previously.

The document concludes by acknowledging that these teachings are only a starting point for deeper reflection on piety, and that each person must adapt these principles to their personal situation.

Chapter 1 - Man's duty in the world

The foundation of piety and the root of complete service is for an individual to clarify and verify his duty in this world and to understand what should guide his outlook and aspirations in all his lifelong endeavors. Our Sages of blessed memory have taught us that humans were created solely to delight in God and bask in the radiance of His Presence, for this is the true delight and the greatest of all pleasures. The place of this delight is truly in the World to Come, which was created specifically for this purpose.

However, the means to reach this desired destination is this world. As our Sages of blessed memory said: "This world is like a vestibule before the World to Come."[1] The means that bring a person to this ultimate purpose are the mitzvot which God, blessed be His Name, has commanded us to perform. These mitzvot can only be performed in this world. Therefore, humans were placed in this world first, so that through these means available here, they can reach the place prepared for them - the World to Come - to delight there in the goodness they acquired through these means. This is what our Sages, of blessed memory, said: "Today is for doing them and tomorrow is for receiving reward." [2]

When you contemplate this matter, you will see that true perfection is only attachment to Him, blessed be He. This is what King David expressed: "But as for me, God's nearness is my good." [3] And he also said: "One thing I ask of the Lord, that I seek - that I may dwell in the House of the Lord all the days of my life, etc."[4] For only this is good, and all that people consider good besides this is vain and deceptive foolishness. However, to merit this goodness, one must first toil and strive with great effort to acquire it. That is, one should strive to attach oneself to Him, blessed be He, through deeds that lead to this goal - namely, the mitzvot.

The Holy One, Blessed be He, has placed humans in a world where many things can distance them from Him, particularly material desires. If one is drawn after these desires, they distance themselves and move away from the true good. Thus, we are truly placed amidst a fierce battle, for all matters of the world, whether for good or bad, are tests for humanity. Poverty on one hand and wealth on the other, as Solomon said: "Lest I become sated and deny and say, 'Who is the Lord?', and lest I become impoverished and steal, etc."[5] Tranquility on one hand and suffering on the other, until the battle is found before and behind us. If one proves to be valorous and triumphs in this war on all sides, they will become the perfect individual who merits attachment to their Creator and emerges from this vestibule to enter the palace, basking in the light of life. To the degree that one conquers their evil inclination and desires, distances themselves from what separates them from the good, and strives to attach themselves to Him, so will they attain Him and rejoice in Him.

Upon deeper reflection, you will see that the world was created for human use. However, it exists in a delicate balance. If a person is drawn after worldly desires and distances themselves from their Creator, they deteriorate and cause the world to deteriorate with them. But if one masters themselves, attaches to their Creator, and uses the world only to assist in serving Him, they elevate themselves and the world is elevated with them. For it is indeed a great elevation for all creatures to be of service to the perfect individual who is sanctified with His sanctity, blessed be He. This is similar to what our Sages, may their memory be for a blessing, said regarding the light that the Holy One, Blessed be He, stored away for the righteous: "When the Holy One, Blessed be He, saw the light that He stored away for the righteous, He rejoiced, as it is stated: 'The light of the righteous will rejoice.'"[6]

Regarding the stones that Yaakov took and placed around his head, they said: "Rebbi Yitzchak said: This teaches that they all gathered together into one place and each one said, 'Upon me the righteous one will rest his head.'"[7]

Our Sages of blessed memory have indeed alerted us to this fundamental principle in the Midrash Kohelet, where they said: "'See the work of God, etc.' When the Holy One, Blessed be He, created Adam the first man, He took him and led him round all the trees of the Garden of Eden and said to him: Behold My works, how beautiful and praiseworthy they are! All that I have created, I created for your sake. Pay attention that you do not corrupt and destroy My world."[8]

The Way to Spiritual Integrity

In summary, humans were not created for their situation in this world, but for their situation in the World to Come. However, their situation in this world is a means to reach their situation in the World to Come, which is the ultimate purpose. Therefore, you will find numerous statements from our Sages, may their memory be for a blessing, all following one style, likening this world to a place and time of preparation, and the World to Come to the place of rest and enjoyment of what has been prepared. This is what they said: "This world is similar to a vestibule"[9], as they said, of blessed memory: "Today is for doing them and tomorrow is for receiving reward"[10]. "One who toiled on Shabbat eve will eat on Shabbat"[11]. "This world is similar to dry land and the World to Come to the sea, etc."[12] There are many such statements along this line.

You can truly see that no intelligent person could believe that the purpose of human creation is for their situation in this world. For what is human life in this world, and who is truly happy and tranquil here? "The days of our years among them are seventy years, and if with might, eighty years; but their pride is toil and pain"[13] - with many types of pain, illnesses, ailments and troubles, and after all this, death. Not one out of a thousand is found for whom the world grants many pleasures and true tranquility, and even such a person, if they live to a hundred years, has already passed and is negated from the world.

Moreover, if the purpose of human creation were for their situation in this world, there would be no need to instill in them such an important and lofty soul that is greater even than the angels themselves, especially since it finds no satisfaction in any worldly pleasures. This is what our Sages taught us, of blessed memory, in Midrash Kohelet: "'And also the soul will not be filled' - To what is this comparable? To a villager who married a princess. If he brings her everything in the world, it is worth nothing to her, for she is a princess. So too the soul - if you bring it all the delicacies of the world, they are nothing to it. Why? Because it comes from above."[14]

Similarly, our Rabbis, may their memory be for a blessing, said: "Against your will you were created and against your will you were born."[15] For the soul does not love this world at all; on the contrary, it despises it. If so, the Creator, blessed be He, certainly would not create a being for a purpose that goes against its nature and is despised by it. Rather, human creation is for their condition in the World to Come. Therefore, this soul was placed in them, for it is fitting for it to serve, and through it humans can receive reward in its place and time, so that nothing despised will befall their soul in this world. On the contrary, it will be loved and cherished by it. This is simple.

Now that we understand this, we immediately grasp the gravity of the mitzvot that are upon us and the preciousness of the service in our hands. For behold, these are the means that bring us to true perfection, without which it cannot be attained at all. However, it is known that the goal is not reached except through the power of assembling all the means that were found and that served to reach it. According to the power of the means and their utilization, so will be the goal born of them. Any slight difference found in the means will certainly be discerned with clarity when the time of the goal born of the assembly of all of them arrives, as I wrote, and this is clear. From now on, it is certain that the precision with which one must approach the mitzvot and service must be of the utmost exactitude, as weighers of gold and pearls are exacting due to their great value. For their outcome is born in true perfection and eternal preciousness, above which there is no greater preciousness.

We have thus learned that the main purpose of human existence in this world is only to fulfill mitzvot, serve, and withstand trials. The pleasures of the world should be for us merely as an aid and assistance, providing contentment and peace of mind to turn our hearts to the service that is incumbent upon us. Indeed, it is fitting that our entire orientation should be only towards the blessed Creator, and we should have no other purpose in any act we perform, small or large, except to draw close to Him, blessed be He, and to break down all the barriers that separate us from our Maker. These are all matters of materiality and what depends on them, until we are drawn after Him, blessed be He, literally like iron after a magnet. Whatever we can think of as a means for this closeness, we should pursue it, grasp it, and not let go of it.

And whatever we can think of as a hindrance to this, we should flee from it as one flees from fire. As it is said: "My soul cleaves after You; Your right hand upholds me."[16] Since our coming to the world is only for this purpose, namely, to attain this closeness by rescuing our soul from all that prevents it and causes it to lose out, now that we know and have clarified for ourselves the truth of this principle, we must examine its details according to their levels, from the beginning of the matter to its end, as Rabbi Pinchas ben Yair arranged them in his statement that we already cited in our introduction. They are: vigilance, zeal, cleanliness, separation, purity, piety, humility, fear of sin, and holiness. Now we will explain them one by one with the help of Heaven.

[1] Avot 4:16
[2] Eruvin 22a
[3] Psalms 73:28
[4] Psalms 27:4
[5] Proverbs 30:9
[6] Chagiga 12a; Proverbs 13:9
[7] Chullin 91b
[8] Kohelet Rabba 7:13
[9] Avot 4:16
[10] Eruvin 22a
[11] Avodah Zara 3a
[12] Kohelet Rabba 1:15
[13] Psalms 90:10
[14] Kohelet Rabba 6:6
[15] Avot 4:22

Chapter 2 - Vigilance

The essence of vigilance is that a person should be careful in their actions and affairs. This means contemplating and supervising one's actions and ways, evaluating whether they are good or not, so as not to abandon one's soul to the danger of perdition, God forbid. One should not walk blindly in the course of habit like a person in darkness. This is a matter that reason certainly demands. For after a person has been granted understanding and intellect to save themselves and flee from the destruction of their soul, how can they want to close their eyes to their own salvation? There is no lesser or more evil folly than this, surely.

One who behaves this way is less than the animals and creatures that, by their nature, guard themselves and therefore flee and escape from everything that appears harmful to them. A person who goes about in their world without contemplating whether their way is good or bad is like a blind person walking on the edge of a river, whose danger is certainly great and whose peril is closer than their salvation.

Indeed, the lack of guarding against natural blindness or willful blindness - that is, deliberately closing one's eyes - amounts to the same thing. Jeremiah lamented the evil of the people of his generation because they were afflicted with this trait. They hid their eyes from their deeds without paying attention to see what should be done or abandoned. He said about them: "No one repented of his wickedness saying etc. They all galloped in their courses like a horse rushing into battle."[1] That is, they pursued and walked in the courses of their feet and their ways without leaving themselves time to examine their actions and ways, and consequently, they fell into evil without seeing it.

This is indeed one of the stratagems of the evil inclination and its cunning - to constantly weigh down its service on the hearts of men until they have no space to contemplate and look at which way they are going. For it knows that if they were to pay a little attention to their ways, they would immediately begin to reconsider their deeds, and remorse would grow and strengthen in them until they would completely abandon sin. This is similar to the advice of the wicked Pharaoh who said: "Let heavier work be laid upon the men etc."[2], as he intended not to leave them any respite at all, so as not to give them attention or allow them to plot against him. Rather, he strove to disturb their hearts from all contemplation by the power of unceasing work. So is the advice of the evil inclination itself to men, for it is a warrior and teaches cunningly, and it is impossible to escape from it except by great wisdom and deep insight.

This is what the prophet cries out and says: "Consider your ways."[3] And Solomon said in his wisdom: "Do not give sleep to your eyes nor slumber to your eyelids, Save yourself like a gazelle from the hand etc."[4] Our Sages of blessed memory said: "All who set their ways in this world merit and see the salvation of the Holy One, blessed be He."[5] It is obvious that even if a person supervises themselves, they cannot be saved unless the Holy One, blessed be He, helps them, for the evil inclination is very strong, as the verse says: "The wicked watches for the righteous and seeks to kill him, the Lord will not leave him etc."[6]

But if a person supervises himself, then the Holy One, blessed be He, helps him and he is saved from the evil inclination. But if he does not supervise himself, surely the Holy One, blessed be He, will not supervise him. For if he does not have mercy, who will have mercy on him? And this is similar to what our Rabbis of blessed memory said: "Anyone who has no understanding, it is forbidden to have mercy on him."[7] And this is what they said: "If I am not for myself, who will be for me."[8]

[1] Jeremiah 8:6
[2] Exodus 5:9
[3] Haggai 1:5-7
[4] Proverbs 6:4-5
[5] Moed Katan 5a; Sotah 5b
[6] Psalms 37:32-33
[7] Berakhot 33a
[8] Avot 1:14

Chapter 3 - Levels of vigilance

Indeed, one who wishes to oversee themselves needs two perspectives: First, to understand what is truly good that a person should choose, and what is truly evil that they should flee from. Second, to examine their actions, both at the time of action and not, to see if they are good or evil.

At the time of action, one should not perform any deed without weighing it on the scale of this knowledge. When not in action, one should recall all their deeds and weigh them as well, to identify what evil is in them so that it may be rejected, and what good is in them to continue and strengthen. If evil is found, one should contemplate and investigate what strategy to employ to turn away from that evil and cleanse oneself from it.

Our Sages of blessed memory have made this matter known to us in their saying: "It would have been better for man not to have been created than to have been created. Now that he has been created, let him examine his deeds. And some say, let him feel his deeds."[1] Note that these two wordings offer two beneficial admonitions. The examining of deeds involves investigating all actions and contemplating them, to see if any should not be done according to God's commandments and statutes, so that these may be eradicated.

The feeling, however, is an investigation even into good deeds themselves, to see if there is any aspect that is not good or some evil part that needs removal. This is like feeling a garment to test if it is strong or worn out; so should one feel their deeds to test their character with ultimate discernment until they remain pure and clean. In principle: a person should carefully examine all their deeds and oversee all their ways to avoid bad habits and character traits, all the more so transgressions and crimes. One should be meticulous and weigh their ways daily, like great merchants who always balance their dealings to avoid spoilage, setting specific times for this so that the weighing is not happenstance, but consistent, for it has many consequences.

The Sages have explicitly taught us the need for this accounting, saying: "Therefore the rulers will say, 'Come, let us calculate' - therefore the rulers of their inclination will say, come and let us calculate the account of the world, the loss of a mitzvah against its reward and the gain of a transgression against its loss," etc.[2] This true counsel can only be given by those who have escaped the grip of their inclination and rule over it. For one still imprisoned by their inclination cannot see this truth, as the inclination blinds their eyes, like one walking in the dark before obstacles they cannot see. As they said: "'You make darkness and it is night' - this is this world which is similar to night."[3]

Understand how profound this saying is for one who delves to understand it. The darkness of night can cause two types of errors to a person's eye: either covering it so that one doesn't see what's before them at all, or fooling them to see a pillar as a person, and a person as a pillar. Similarly, the materialism of this world is darkness for the mind's eye, causing two errors: First, it prevents one from seeing obstacles in life's ways, and fools go securely, falling and perishing without fear. As Scripture says: "The way of the wicked is like darkness; they do not know what they stumble over."[4] It says: "A prudent man sees evil and hides himself, but the simple go on and suffer."[5] And: "The fool rageth and is confident"[6], for their heart seems sound to them as a great hall, and they fall before recognizing the obstacle.

The second mistake, more difficult than the first, is that it distorts their vision until they see bad as good, and good as bad, strengthening them in evil deeds. Not only do they lack sight of truth to see the evil before them, but they find seeming proofs for their false views, a great evil that leads them to destruction. As the verse says: "Make the heart of this people fat, and make their ears heavy, and shut their eyes; lest they see with their eyes," etc.[7] All this is because they are under darkness and ruled by their inclination. But those who have left this prison see the truth as it is and can advise others.

This is comparable to a maze garden, planted for amusement, where walls of plantings create confusing paths, all similar, with the goal to reach a central pavilion. Some paths are straight and reach the pavilion, while others lead astray. One walking these paths cannot discern the true from the false, for they all appear the same, unless they know the way from experience. One who stands on the pavilion sees all paths and can warn others, saying, "This is the way, walk in it!" Those who believe will reach the destination, while those who follow their own eyes will remain lost.

The Way to Spiritual Integrity

So it is with this matter: One who hasn't mastered their inclination is amid the paths, unable to discern between them. But those who rule over their inclination, having reached the pavilion and left the paths, see all ways clearly and can advise others. We must believe them. What advice do they give? "Come, let us calculate," let us calculate the account of the world, for they have experienced and know that this alone is the true way to reach the good one seeks.

The main point is that a person must constantly contemplate, at all times and during set times of seclusion, what is the true path according to the Torah in which one must walk. Afterwards, one should examine their deeds to see if they align with this path. Through this, one will find it easier to cleanse themselves of evil and straighten their ways. As Scripture says: "Ponder the path of your feet, and let all your ways be established."[8] And: "Let us search and try our ways, and turn back to the Lord."[9]

[1] Eruvin 13b
[2] Bava Batra 78b
[3] Bava Metzia 83b; Psalms 104:20
[4] Proverbs 4:19
[5] Proverbs 22:3
[6] Proverbs 14:16
[7] Isaiah 6:10
[8] Proverbs 4:26
[9] Lamentations 3:40

Chapter 4 - Acquiring vigilance

What generally brings a person to the way of caution is the study of Torah. This is what Rabbi Pinchas said at the beginning of the Baraita, "Torah leads to caution."[1] However, what specifically leads to this is contemplating the gravity of the service that a person is obligated in, and the depth of the judgement upon it. This comes from examining the deeds written in the holy books and from studying the sayings of the Sages of blessed memory that arouse one to this.

There are levels of contemplation for different groups: those of perfect understanding, those lesser than them, and the masses as a whole. For those of perfect understanding, the contemplation will be in realizing that only perfection is worthy of desire, and there is no greater evil than lacking perfection or being distanced from it. Once this becomes clear to them, along with the understanding that good deeds and character traits are the means to perfection, they will never want to lessen these means or treat them lightly. They will realize that if these means are lessened or weakened, they will not attain true perfection, but it will be diminished according to how much they diminished their efforts. Therefore, they will choose to increase their efforts and be stringent in all conditions, never resting from worry lest something be lacking that will prevent them from achieving the perfection they desire. This is what King Solomon meant when he said, "Happy is the man who is always reverent,"[2] which the Sages explained as referring to matters of Torah.[3]

The highest level of this is what's called fear of sin, one of the most praiseworthy levels. This is when a person is always afraid and worried lest some trace of sin be found in their actions that will prevent them from achieving the perfection they're obligated to strive for. About this, the Sages said in a parable, "This teaches that each one is singed by the canopy of his fellow."[4] This isn't due to jealousy, which only affects those lacking understanding, but because one sees oneself lacking a level of perfection that could have been attained, just as their fellow attained it. Based on this contemplation, one who is perfect in understanding will certainly be cautious in their deeds.

For those of lesser understanding, the contemplation will be according to their discernment, particularly in terms of the honor they desire. It's obvious to anyone of understanding that levels in the World to Come are apportioned according to deeds. Only one who has greater deeds than their fellow will be elevated there, while one with few deeds will be lowly. How then can a person close their eyes to their deeds or lessen their efforts, knowing it will pain them later when they can't repair what they've corrupted?

There are fools who seek to make things easy for themselves, saying, "Why should we exert ourselves with so much piety and asceticism? Isn't it enough not to be among the wicked sentenced to Gehinnom? We won't force ourselves to enter the innermost part of the Garden of Eden. If we have a small portion, that's enough for us." However, let's ask them: In this transient world, could they easily bear seeing one of their fellows, or even a servant or poor person, more honored and exalted than them without pain and inner turmoil? Certainly not! We see that all of man's toil is to be elevated over others and to place himself among those higher than him, for it is "a man's envy of his neighbor".[5] If it's so difficult for them to be lower than others in imaginary and false attributes, how will they bear seeing themselves more lowly than those very people who are now lower than them in a place of true virtue and eternal value?

This indulgence they seek to lighten their burden of service is nothing but a false enticement from their inclination, not a true matter at all. There would be no place for this enticement if they saw the truth of the matter. But since they don't seek it and go astray willingly, this enticement won't depart from them until it's too late to repair what they've corrupted. King Solomon said, "Whatever your hand finds to do, do with your might; for there is no work, nor device, nor knowledge, nor wisdom, in Sheol, where you are going."[6] What a person doesn't do while they have the power of free choice given by the Creator, they won't be able to do in the grave. One who didn't increase good deeds in life can't do them afterwards. One who didn't account for their deeds won't have time to do so then. One who didn't gain wisdom in this world won't gain it in the grave.

For the masses, the contemplation is in terms of reward and punishment themselves, seeing how far the depth of judgment reaches. One should constantly tremble over this, for who can stand on the day of judgment and be justified before the Creator when His gaze examines every small and great matter? Our Rabbis said, "'And makes known to man what is his thought' - even the lightest conversation between a man and his wife is told to a person at the time of judgment."[7]

They further said, "'And around Him it storms mightily' - this teaches that the Holy One, Blessed be He, is exacting with His pious ones to a hairsbreadth."[8]

Even great figures like Abraham, Jacob, Joseph, David, and others weren't exempted from judgment for slight matters. The Sages provide numerous examples of how even small missteps or seemingly insignificant actions led to consequences for these revered figures.

Rabbi Yochanan would cry when he reached the verse, "'And I will draw near to you for judgment, and I will be a swift witness,' etc."[19] A servant whose Master reckons his minor sins as major ones - does he have a remedy? This doesn't mean the punishment for both is the same, for God repays measure for measure. Rather, in weighing deeds, minor ones count as much as major ones. The major ones don't cause the minor ones to be forgotten, and the Judge doesn't overlook them. He oversees all with the same perspective, judging each and punishing afterwards according to what it is.

King Solomon says, "For God will bring every deed into judgment," etc.[20] Just as God doesn't refrain from remembering every small good deed, He also doesn't refrain from judging every small evil deed. This removes the idea that God will not bring minor matters into His judgments. The general rule is, "Anyone who says the Holy One, Blessed be He, is forgiving, his life will be forgiven."[21]

Moses said, "The Rock, His work is perfect, for all His ways are justice; a God of faithfulness and without iniquity, just and right is He."[23] Since God wants justice, He must give to each according to their ways and the fruit of their doings with ultimate precision, whether for good or bad. The attribute of mercy, while essential for the world's sustenance, doesn't impair justice. It provides three things: time for the sinner instead of immediate destruction, punishment that isn't utter destruction, and the opportunity for repentance. When a penitent truly regrets their sin and changes their ways, the uprooting of the will is considered like the uprooting of the deed.

However, for transgressions to be permitted without anything or for God to ignore them would be completely against justice. If one of the ways mentioned for the sinner to escape isn't found, the attribute of justice will not return empty-handed. As the Sages said, "He is long-suffering and collects His due."[27]

In conclusion, there is no enticement by which a person who wants to open their eyes can be enticed to not be cautious in their deeds with the utmost caution and be exacting in them with the utmost precision. Contemplating all these perspectives and acquiring through them the trait of caution is definite, if one is a person of soul.

[1] Avodah Zarah 20b

[2] Proverbs 28:14

[3] Berachot 60a

[4] Bava Batra 75a

[5] Ecclesiastes 4:4

[6] Ecclesiastes 9:10

[7] Chagigah 5b; Amos 4:13

[8] Yevamot 121b; Bava Kamma 50a; Psalms 50:3

[9] Isaiah 41:8

[10] Genesis 15:8; Genesis Rabbah 44:18

[11] Genesis Rabbah 54:4

[12] Genesis 30:1; Genesis Rabbah 71:7

[13] Job 6:14

[14] Genesis Rabbah 76:9; ibid. 80:4

[15] Genesis 40:14; Genesis Rabbah 89:2-3

[16] Sotah 35a

[17] II Samuel 6:23

[18] II Kings 20:18

[19] Chagigah 5a; Malachi 3:5

[20] Ecclesiastes 12:14

[21] Bava Kamma 50a

[22] Jeremiah 10:10

[23] Deuteronomy 32:4

[24] Isaiah 6:7

[25] Sanhedrin 104a

[26] Ecclesiastes Rabbah 7:27

[27] Jerusalem Talmud Shekalim 5:1; Jerusalem Talmud Beitzah 3:8; Jerusalem Talmud Taanit 2:1

Chapter 5 - Destructive causes of vigilance

Indeed, there are three main factors that destroy and distance one from the quality of vigilance: worldly involvement and preoccupation, laughter and scoffing, and bad company. Let's examine each of these in turn.

We've already discussed worldly involvement and preoccupation. When a person is consumed by worldly matters, their thoughts are bound by the chains of these burdens, making it impossible to pay proper attention to their deeds. Recognizing this, our sages advised, "Minimize your business pursuits and engage in Torah."[1] While business is necessary for livelihood, excessive business shouldn't leave no room for one's service to God. We're therefore commanded to set fixed times for Torah study, which is crucial for attaining vigilance. As Rabbi Pinchas said, "Torah leads to vigilance"[2], and without it, one cannot attain it at all. This is why our sages stated, "An ignoramus cannot be a pious person."[3]

The Creator, who created the evil inclination in man, also created the Torah as its antidote. As our sages said, "I created the evil inclination; I created the Torah as its antidote."[4] It's clear that if the Creator provided no other remedy for this ailment, it's impossible to be cured without it. Anyone who thinks they can be saved without it is mistaken and will realize their error when they die in sin. The evil inclination is incredibly strong in a person, often intensifying and dominating without one's knowledge. If one tries every trick in the world but doesn't use the prescribed remedy - the Torah - they won't even realize how their illness has worsened until it's too late.

This is comparable to a sick person who consults doctors, receives a diagnosis and prescription, but then ignores the prescribed medicine in favor of remedies of their own choosing. Won't that patient surely die? Similarly, no one understands the illness of the evil inclination and its ingrained power except its Creator, who warned us that the Torah is its remedy. Who then would abandon it for other solutions and expect to live? The darkness of materialism will intensify gradually, and one may find themselves sunk in evil and far removed from truth, not even considering seeking it. But if one engages in Torah study, seeing its ways, commands, and warnings, an awakening will naturally occur, leading them to the good path. As our sages said, "Would that they abandoned Me but kept My Torah, for the light within it would return them to the good."[5]

This also includes setting fixed times for self-reflection and correction of one's deeds. If one has free time from business pursuits, wisdom dictates using it immediately for the pursuit of one's soul and the improvement of one's service to God. While this destroyer is the most common, it's also the easiest to escape for those who truly wish to do so.

The second destroyer, laughter and scoffing, is much more difficult to overcome. One immersed in these is like someone drowning in a vast sea, from which escape is extremely challenging. Laughter destroys a person's heart, stripping away taste and knowledge. Such a person becomes like a drunk or a fool, impossible to guide or counsel. As King Solomon said, "Of laughter I said, 'It is mad,' and of mirth, 'What good is it?'"[6] Our sages warned, "Laughter and frivolity accustom a person to licentiousness."[7] Even though licentiousness is severe in the eyes of every intelligent person, laughter and frivolity gradually draw one closer to it, removing fear little by little until one reaches the sin itself.

Why is this so? Just as vigilance depends on paying attention, the essence of laughter is removing the heart from upright and contemplative thoughts. Consequently, thoughts of fear don't enter the heart at all.

The destructive power of scoffing is particularly severe. Like an oil-smeared shield that deflects arrows, scoffing deflects rebuke and chastisement. With a single jest or small laugh, a person can nullify a great deal of arousal and impact that the heart would otherwise experience when encountering matters that prompt self-reflection. Scoffing's power destroys all matters of morality and fear, not because of the weakness of these matters or lack of understanding, but due to scoffing's destructive nature.
The prophet Isaiah lamented this, seeing how it prevented his rebukes from making an impression and ruined hope for sinners. He warned, "Now, do not scoff, lest your bonds be tightened."[8] Our sages have decreed that the scoffer brings suffering upon himself[9], as the verse explicitly states, "Penalties are prepared for scoffers."[10] This is what justice dictates: one who is impressed by contemplation and teachings

doesn't need physical punishment, as they'll repent through the thoughts of repentance born from moral lessons. But scoffers, unimpressed by rebukes due to their scoffing, can only be corrected through penalties. The true Judge was stringent in punishment according to the severity of the sin and its consequences. Our sages taught, "Scoffing is severe, for its beginning is suffering and its end is destruction."[11]

The third detrimental factor is bad company, particularly the company of fools and sinners. As the verse states, "He who walks with the wise grows wise, but a companion of fools suffers harm."[12] We often see that even after acknowledging their duty to serve and be vigilant, people may become lax or transgress to avoid ridicule from peers or to fit in. Solomon warns against this, saying, "Do not associate with those given to change."[13]

If someone argues, "One should always be agreeable with people,"[14] respond that this applies to those who behave like humans, not those who act like animals. Solomon further advises, "Stay away from a foolish man."[15]

King David said, "Blessed is the man who does not walk in the counsel of the wicked."[16] Our Sages interpreted: "If he walks[with them], he will eventually stand[with them]. If he stands, he will eventually sit[with them]."[17] He also states, "I do not sit with deceitful men... I abhor the assembly of evildoers."[18] One should purify oneself, avoiding the ways of those immersed in worldly vanities, and turn towards God's courts. David concludes, "I wash my hands in innocence, and go about your altar, Lord."[19]

If one finds oneself among mockers, one should disregard their derision. Instead, one should mock the mockers and despise them, reasoning: "If I had the opportunity to earn a large sum, would I forgo it because of mockery? How much more so should I not want to lose my soul because of it!"

Our Sages advised, "Be bold as a leopard... to do the will of your Father in heaven."[20] David said, "I will speak of your statutes before kings and will not be put to shame."[21] Although most kings discuss matters of grandeur and pleasure, David, being a king himself, might have been embarrassed to speak of moral and Torah matters in their company. Yet he did not care about this at all. His heart was not enticed by these vanities after grasping the truth. Similarly, Isaiah said, "I have set my face like flint, and I know I will not be put to shame."[22]

[1] Avot 4:10

[2] Avodah Zarah 20b

[3] Avot 2:5

[4] Kiddushin 30b

[5] Jerusalem Talmud Chagigah 1:7; Lamentations Rabbah Proems; Yalkut Shimoni Jeremiah, Remez 282

[6] Ecclesiastes 2:2

[7] Avot 3:13

[8] Isaiah 28:22

[9] Avodah Zarah 18b

[10] Proverbs 19:29

[11] Avodah Zarah 18b; Isaiah 28:22

[12] Proverbs 13:20

[13] Proverbs 24:21

[14] Ketubot 17a

[15] Proverbs 14:7

[16] Psalms 1:1

[17] Avodah Zarah 18b

[18] Psalms 26:4-5

[19] Psalms 26:6

[20] Avot 5:20

[21] Psalms 119:46

[22] Isaiah 50:7

Chapter 6 – Zeal - Diligence

After caution comes zeal. While caution pertains to "do not do," zeal relates to "do," as it is written, "Turn from evil and do good."[1] The essence of zeal is clear: it is the prelude to fulfilling commandments and completing their purpose. Our Sages said, "The zealous are early in performing commandments."[2]

Just as great vigilance and extensive observation are needed to escape the snares of the evil inclination and prevent evil from infiltrating our actions, they are equally necessary to grasp the commandments, merit them, and not lose them. The evil inclination not only schemes to make a person fall into sin but also strives to prevent them from performing commandments. If one is lax and lazy, not strengthening oneself to pursue and hold onto them, one will certainly remain devoid of them.

Human nature is inherently heavy due to the coarseness of materiality. Therefore, people naturally shy away from toil and labor. One who wants to merit serving the Creator must overcome their own nature, strengthen themselves, and be zealous. If one succumbs to their own heaviness, they will surely not succeed. This is what the Sage said, "Be bold as a leopard, light as an eagle, swift as a deer, and strong as a lion to do the will of your Father in heaven."[3] Similarly, our Sages counted among the things that require strengthening: Torah and good deeds.[4] It is an explicit verse, "Be strong and very courageous to observe to do according to all the Torah which Moses My servant commanded you."[5] For great strength is needed to overcome nature to its opposite.

Solomon repeatedly warned about this, seeing the evil of laziness and the great loss that comes from it. He said, "A little sleep, a little slumber, a little folding of the hands to rest — and poverty will come on you like a thief and scarcity like an armed man."[6] The lazy person brings evil upon themselves through inaction. He also said, "One who is slack in his work is brother to one who destroys."[7] Even though he is not the active destroyer, do not think he is far from it; rather, he is its brother and peer.

He further illustrated the evil of the lazy person with a vivid image: "I went past the field of a sluggard, past the vineyard of someone who has no sense; thorns had come up everywhere, the ground was covered with weeds, and the stone wall was in ruins. I applied my heart to what I observed and learned a lesson from what I saw: A little sleep, a little slumber, a little folding of the hands to rest — and poverty will come on you like a thief and scarcity like an armed man."[8]

Besides its literal meaning, our Sages interpreted it allegorically: "'Thorns had come up everywhere' — he seeks an explanation of a Torah portion but does not find it. 'The ground was covered with weeds' — because he did not labor in them, he sits and declares the pure impure and the impure pure, and breaches the fences of the wise. What is the punishment for this?

Solomon explained it: 'Whoever breaks through a wall may be bitten by a snake.'"[9]

The evil of the lazy person does not come all at once, but gradually, without them realizing it. They are drawn from one evil to another until they find themselves immersed in the depths of evil. At first, it's merely a lack of necessary effort, which leads to insufficient Torah study. Due to this lack of study, when they later attempt to learn, they lack understanding.

If their evil ended there, it would already be significant. But it continues to grow when, wanting to understand that Torah portion anyway, they reveal incorrect interpretations, corrupting the truth and inverting it, transgressing the ordinances and breaching the fences. Their end is destruction, as is the judgment of all who breach fences. Solomon said, "I applied my heart to what I observed,"[10] meaning, "I contemplated this matter and saw the greatness of its evil, which is like a venom that spreads gradually, and its effect is not noticeable until death." This is the meaning of "A little sleep..."[11]

We often see that even after a person's heart knows their duty and the truth has been established regarding what is appropriate to save their soul and what is their duty from their Creator, nevertheless they abandon it. This is not due to a lack of recognition of that duty, nor for any other reason, but because the heaviness of laziness overcomes them. They say, "I will eat a little," or "I will sleep a little," or "It is difficult for me to leave my house," "I have taken off my robe, how can I put it on?" "The sun is too strong," "The cold is too great," or "It's raining," and all the other excuses that the lazy are full of. In the meantime, the Torah is neglected, the service of God is canceled, and the person forsakes their Creator. This is what Solomon says "Through laziness the rafters sag, and through idleness the house leaks."[12]

But if you ask the lazy person, they will come to you with many sayings of the sages, verses from the scriptures, and claims from reason, all of which will instruct them, according to their distorted opinion, to be lenient with themselves and remain in their laziness. They do not see that these claims and reasons are not born from discretion, but flow from the source of their laziness. For when laziness prevails in them, it inclines their mind and intellect to these claims, which will not listen to the voice of the wise and those of correct knowledge. This is what Solomon cries out and says "The lazy person is wiser in his own eyes than seven people who give a sensible response."[13] For laziness does not allow them to even pay attention to the words of those who rebuke them, but they consider them all to be erring and foolish, and they alone wise.

Know that this is a great principle, proven in the craft of abstinence, that every leniency needs examination. For even though it may be upright and correct, it is likely that it is from the counsel of the evil inclination and its deceptions. Therefore, it is necessary to examine it with many inquiries and investigations. If after all these it is righteous, it is certainly good.

In sum, a person needs great strengthening to overcome laziness and perform the commandments with diligence. You will see that the angels were praised for this good quality, as it is said about them "mighty in strength, who perform His word, hearkening to the sound of His word."[14] And it says "And the living beings sped back and forth like bolts of lightning."[15] Man is man and not an angel, so it is impossible for him to reach the strength of an angel. But certainly, as much as he can approach this level, he should approach. King David would praise his lot and say "I hurried and did not delay to keep Your commandments."[16]

[1] Psalms 34:15

[2] Pesachim 4a; Yoma 28b

[3] Avot 5:20

[4] Berachot 32b

[5] Joshua 1:7

[6] Proverbs 6:10; 24:33-34

[7] Proverbs 18:9

[8] Proverbs 24:30-34

[9] Yalkut Shimoni, Proverbs 961; Ecclesiastes 10:8

[10] Proverbs 24:32

[11] Proverbs 24:33-34

[12] Ecclesiastes 10:18

[13] Proverbs 26:16

[14] Psalms 103:20

[15] Ezekiel 1:14

[16] Psalms 119:60

Chapter 7 - Degrees of zeal

Zeal or Diligence consists of two parts: one before the deed and one after it. Before starting the deed, one should not miss the opportunity to perform a commandment. When its time comes, or it presents itself, or it comes to mind, one should hasten to grasp and do it without delay. For there is no danger like the danger of delay, as every passing moment brings the potential for new hindrances to the good deed.

Our sages alerted us to this truth regarding Solomon's coronation. When David said to Benaiah, "Take him down to Gihon," and Benaiah answered, "Amen! May the Lord say so," they commented: "Rabbi Pinchas in the name of Rabbi Hanan of Tzippori: But is it not already stated, 'Behold, a son will be born to you; he will be a man of rest'? Rather, many accusers might arise between here and Gihon"[1]. Therefore, our sages warned, "And you shall observe the commandments," and "A commandment that comes to your hand, do not let it leaven." They also said, "A person should always precede others in a matter of a commandment, for since the elder[Rachel] preceded the younger[Leah], she merited and preceded her by four generations to the kingship in Israel"[2].

They stated, "The diligent precede others to the commandments"[3], and "A person should always run to a matter of a commandment, even on the Sabbath"[4]. In a midrash they said, "'He leads me in the paths of righteousness for His name's sake,' 'With diligence, like these young women, as you say, 'In the midst of maidens playing timbrels.'" Diligence is a quality of great perfection, which human nature now hinders. Whoever overcomes this and grasps diligence as much as they can will truly merit it in the future, for the Creator will give it to them as a reward for their striving during their time of service.

Diligence after starting the deed means that once one has begun a commandment, they should hasten to complete it. They should not take it lightly or treat it as a burden to be thrown off, but rather act out of fear that they might not merit to complete it. Our sages exhorted much about this, saying, "Anyone who starts a commandment and does not finish it buries his wife and children." They also said, "A commandment is only called by the name of the one who completes it"[5].

King Solomon said, "Do you see a man skilled in his work? He will stand before kings; he will not stand before obscure men." The sages attributed this praise to Solomon because he hastened in building the Temple without delay. They also praised Moses for his haste in constructing the Tabernacle[6].

You'll find that all the deeds of the righteous are done with haste. About Abraham, it's written, "And Abraham hastened into the tent to Sarah, and said, 'Make ready quickly, etc.' and he gave it to the young man, who hastened." About Rebecca, "And she hastened and emptied her pitcher, etc." They said in a midrash, "'And the woman hastened, etc.,' 'This teaches that all the deeds of the righteous are done with haste'"[7]. They do not delay either in beginning or completing a commandment.

A person whose soul burns in the service of their Creator will certainly not be lazy in performing His commandments. Their movement will be like that of a rapid fire, not resting until the matter is completed. Moreover, just as diligence results from inner burning, diligence also generates inner burning. Whoever feels themselves hastening in the performance of a commandment causes their inner movement to burn as well, intensifying desire and delight. But if one moves heavily in their limbs, their spirit's movement will also sink and be extinguished. This is something experience will attest to.

What's most desirable in the service of the Creator is the heart's desire and the soul's longing. King David takes pride in this, saying, "As a hart longs for streams of water, so my soul longs for You, O God," "My soul thirsts for God, etc. My soul yearns, indeed it pines, for the courts of the Lord," "My soul thirsts for You, my flesh longs for You"[8]. For a person in whom this desire doesn't burn properly, good advice is to be intentionally diligent, so that desire will naturally be born from this. External movement arouses the internal, and the external is certainly more under one's control than the internal. By utilizing what is in their control, they can subsequently acquire what isn't, as inner joy, desire, and longing will be born from their chosen enthusiastic movement.

This is what the prophet would say, "Let us know, let us strive to know the Lord," and it is written, "They will follow the Lord; He will roar like a lion"[9].

[1]: I Kings 1:33, Bereishit Rabbah 76:2

[2]: Exodus 12:17, Nazir 23b; Bava Kamma 38b; Horayot 11a

[3]: Pesachim 4a

[4]: Berachot 6

[5]: Bereishit Rabbah 85:3; Sotah 13b, Proverbs 22:29, Sanhedrin 104b

[6]: Shir HaShirim Rabbah 1:2

[7]: Genesis 18:6, Genesis 24:20, Bamidbar Rabbah 10:5, Judges 13:10

[8]: Psalms 42:2, Psalms 84:3, Psalms 63:2

[9]: Hosea 6:3, Hosea 11:10

Chapter 8 - Acquiring zeal

The means by which we acquire zeal are the same as those by which we acquire vigilance, and their levels are similar. As mentioned earlier, these concepts are closely related, differing only in that one applies to positive commandments and the other to negative commandments. When a person realizes the great value of the commandments and their significant obligation, their heart will naturally be stirred to service and they will not slack in it.

What can further increase this arousal is contemplating the many favors that the Holy One, Blessed be He, does for a person at all times and at every hour, and the great wonders He performs from birth until the last day. The more one reflects on these things, the more one will recognize their great obligation to the benevolent God. These reflections will serve as means to prevent laziness and slacking in His service. Since one certainly cannot repay His blessed goodness, at least they can give thanks to His name and fulfill His commandments.

There is no person, regardless of their situation - whether poor or rich, healthy or sick - who does not witness wonders and many favors in their circumstances. The rich and healthy are indebted to Him for their wealth and health. The poor are indebted to Him for miraculously providing their livelihood even in poverty and not letting them die of hunger. The sick are indebted to Him for sustaining them in their severe illness and afflictions and not letting them descend to the pit. In this manner, there is no person who does not recognize themselves as indebted to their Creator.

When one contemplates these favors received from Him, they will certainly be aroused to be quick in His service. This is even more so if one ponders that all their well-being depends on His blessed hand, and what they need and are compelled to have comes from Him, not from another. Therefore, they will certainly not be lazy in serving Him and will not lack what they are compelled to have.

Note that this includes the three levels divided in vigilance, for their matter is essentially one. For those of perfect knowledge, the arousal will come from the aspect of obligation and the value of the deeds and their importance. For those lesser than them, it will come from the aspect of the World to Come and its honor, so that they will not be ashamed on the day of retribution when seeing the goodness, they could have attained and lost. For the masses, it will come from the aspect of this world and its needs, as explained earlier

Chapter 9 - Hindrances to zeal

The detriments of zeal are the same as those that increase laziness. The greatest of them all is seeking physical rest, hating exertion, and loving luxuries with all their conditions. Such a person will certainly find service to their Creator to be a great burden. For one who wants to eat their meals in complete tranquility, sleep undisturbed, walk only at leisure, and similar things - it will be difficult to rise early for synagogue, shorten meals for afternoon prayer, or go out for a mitzvah if the time is inconvenient. All the more so to hasten for matters of mitzvah or Torah study. One who accustoms themselves to these practices is not master of themselves to do the opposite when they want, for their will is already bound in the habit that becomes second nature.

However, a person must know that they are not in this world for rest, but for toil and exertion. They should conduct themselves like workers who labor for their employers, as it is said, "We are day laborers."[1] They should be like soldiers in formation, eating in haste, sleeping temporarily, always ready for battle. As it is said, "For man is born for toil."[2] When one accustoms themselves to this way, they will certainly find service easy, as they will not lack the readiness and preparation for it. Our Sages said, "This is the way of Torah - eat bread with salt, drink water in small measure, sleep on the ground."[3] This is the principle of utmost distancing from rest and luxuries.

Another hindrance to zeal is great fear and trepidation of time and its consequences. One might fear cold or heat, afflictions, illnesses, wind, and so on. Solomon said, "The lazy one says, 'There is a lion on the road, a lion in the streets!'"[4] The Sages have disparaged this trait and attributed it to sinners, as it is written, "The sinners in Zion are afraid; trembling has seized the godless."[5] One great sage even told his student when he saw him being afraid, "You have sinned"[6]. Rather, it is said, "Trust in the Lord and do good; dwell in the land and cultivate faithfulness."[7]

The principle is that a person should consider themselves temporary in the world and permanent in service. They should be content with what comes to them in worldly matters, taking from what comes into their hand. They should be far from rest and close to work and toil, with their heart ready, trusting in the Lord. They should not fear the consequences of time and its afflictions.

One might ask about the Sages' obligation to guard oneself carefully and not place oneself in danger, even for the righteous. They said, "Everything is in the hands of Heaven except for chills and fever."[8] Scripture writes, "And you shall guard yourselves very well."[9] This trust should not be absolute, even for a mitzvah matter.

Know that there is proper fear and foolish fear, trust and folly. The Blessed Lord made man with sound intellect and proper reasoning to conduct himself well and avoid harmful things created to punish the wicked. One who doesn't conduct themselves wisely and exposes themselves to dangers isn't practicing trust but folly. They sin against the Creator's will, who wants man to protect himself. Caution and fear based on wise conduct are appropriate, as it is said, "The prudent sees danger and hides, but the simple go on and suffer for it."[10] But foolish fear is when one adds excessive caution and fear, creating safeguards upon safeguards that lead to neglect of Torah and worship.

The general rule to distinguish between these types of fear is what the sages said: "Where harm is common, it is different."[11] Where harm is known and common, one must be cautious. But where harm is not known, there's no need to fear. As they said, "An unseen blemish is not considered a blemish,"[12] and a wise person only relies on what their eyes see.

The sages explained how foolish fear can deter a person from good deeds: "Solomon mentioned seven things about the sluggard: They said to the sluggard, 'Your teacher is in the city, go and learn Torah from him,' and he replies, 'I am afraid of the lion on the way.' 'Your teacher is within the city,' he says, 'I am afraid there might be a lion in the streets.' They say, 'He is in your home,' he says, 'If I go to him, I will find the door locked,' etc."[13] This shows that it's not fear causing laziness, but laziness causing fear.

Diligence is fitting to be in a higher degree than caution because generally, a person won't be diligent unless they're cautious first. One who doesn't pay attention to their actions and reflect on their service, which is the trait of caution, will find it hard to cultivate love and desire for it and act with zeal in devotion to their Creator. They're still immersed in bodily desires and habitual pursuits that distance them from all this. However, once they've opened their eyes to see their actions and be cautious with them, considering the balance of commandments and sins, it becomes easy to turn away from evil, yearn for good, and act with zeal towards it.

[1] Eruvin 65a
[2] Job 5:7
[3] Avot 6:4
[4] Proverbs 26:13
[5] Isaiah 33:14
[6] Berakhot 60a
[7] Psalms 37:3
[8] Ketubot 30a
[9] Deuteronomy 4:15
[10]: Proverbs 22:3
[11]: Pesachim 8b
[12]: Chullin 56b
[13]: Devarim Rabbah 8:6

Chapter 10 - Cleanliness

The trait of cleanliness is for a person to be completely free from every bad trait and sin. This applies not only to obvious and publicized sins but also to matters the heart is enticed to permit. Upon true investigation, we find that such permissiveness appears only because the heart is still somewhat afflicted by desire, not having been completely purified. Therefore, it will pull one to be lenient with oneself. However, a person who has been completely purified from this affliction and is clean from any evil impression left by desire will have completely clear vision and pure discernment. Desire will not mislead them to anything; rather, they will recognize even the slightest sin as evil and distance themselves from it. Our Sages referred to such perfect individuals who thoroughly purify their deeds as "The pure-minded of Jerusalem"[1].

Now you can see the difference between the vigilant person and the clean one, even though they are close in nature. The vigilant one is careful in their deeds and avoids sinning in matters known and publicized as sins. However, they are not yet master of themselves to the extent that their heart will not be drawn by natural desire, which might mislead them to see permissibility in some matters whose evil is not widely recognized. This is because even though they strive to subdue their inclination and subjugate their desires, this effort doesn't change their nature. They cannot remove physical desire from their heart but rather subdue it and follow wisdom instead.

Nevertheless, the desire for materiality still does its part to incite and entice them.

However, after a person greatly accustoms themselves to this vigilance until they are initially cleansed from publicized sins, and they habituate themselves to service and its zeal, and the love for their Creator and desire for Him overcomes them, the power of this habit will distance them from matters of materiality. It will attach their mind to the perfection of the soul until they can ultimately reach complete cleanliness. The fire of physical desire will be extinguished from their heart with the overcoming of the divine desire within them. Then their vision will remain pure and clear, as mentioned earlier, so that their desire for materiality will not entice or affect them. They will be thoroughly cleansed in their deeds.

Regarding this trait, David would rejoice in himself and say, "I wash my hands in cleanliness, and I go around Your altar, O Lord."[2] For in truth, only one who is completely cleansed from any trace of sin and iniquity is fit to see the face of the King, the Lord. Otherwise, one can only be ashamed and humiliated before Him. As Ezra the Scribe said, "O my God, I am ashamed and humiliated to lift my face to You, my God."[3]

It is certainly a great task for a person to reach the perfection of this trait. The revealed and known transgressions are easier to be careful of since their evil is obvious. But the exactness needed for cleanliness is more difficult because permissibility can conceal sin, as mentioned earlier. It's like what they said,

"The transgressions that a person treads with his heels surround him at the time of judgment."[4] Similarly, they said, "Most of them with theft, and a minority of them with sexual immorality, and all of them with the dust of evil speech."[5] Because of its great subtlety, all people stumble in it as they do not recognize it.

They said that David was careful and cleansed himself completely from all these. Therefore, he would go to war with strong trust, and he would ask, "I pursue my enemies and overtake them, and I do not return until they are destroyed."[6] Which Jehoshaphat, Asa, and Hezekiah did not ask, because they were not as cleansed. This is what he himself said, "The Lord repays me according to my righteousness, according to the cleanness of my hands He recompenses me."[7] He further said, "And the Lord has recompensed me according to my righteousness, according to the cleanness of my hands before His eyes."[8] This is the cleanness and purity we mentioned. Then he went on to say, "For by You I run upon a troop, etc. I pursue my enemies and overtake them."[9] He himself further said, "Who may ascend the mountain of the Lord? Who may stand in His holy place? He who has clean hands and a pure heart."[10]

Certainly, this trait is difficult to achieve, for human nature is weak and the heart is easily enticed, permitting things in which it can find some deception. One who has reached this trait has already attained a great level, for they have stood before a strong battle and prevailed. Now we will proceed to explain the details of this trait.

[1] Sanhedrin 23a
[2] Psalms 26:6
[3] Ezra 9:6
[4] Avodah Zarah 18a
[5] Bava Batra 165a
[6] Psalms 18:38
[7] Psalms 18:21
[8] Psalms 18:25
[9] Psalms 18:30
[10] Psalms 24:3-4

Chapter 11 - Aspects of Cleanliness

The details of the trait of cleanliness are numerous, encompassing all 365 negative commandments. As mentioned earlier, this trait involves being clean from all branches of transgressions. Although the evil inclination strives to cause a person to sin in all transgressions, some are more naturally desirable. With these, it presents more apparent permissibilities, requiring greater strength to overcome one's inclination and be cleansed from sin. As our Sages said, "Theft and sexual immorality, a person's soul desires them and lusts for them"[1].

We observe that while most people are not openly thieves, many still taste the flavor of theft in their business dealings by permitting themselves to profit through another's loss. They say, "To profit is different." However, many prohibitions were stated regarding theft: "You shall not oppress," "You shall not steal," "You shall not steal, and you shall not deal falsely, and you shall not lie to one another," "You shall not wrong one another," "You shall not move your neighbor's boundary." These are all legal distinctions in theft, including many actions common in general commerce, all containing numerous prohibitions.

It's not only the obvious and publicized actions of oppression and theft that are prohibited. Anything that ultimately leads to it is included in the prohibition. Regarding this, they said, "'And he has not defiled his neighbor's wife' (Ezekiel 18:6) - that he did not encroach upon his fellow's livelihood"[2]. Rabbi Judah prohibited a shopkeeper from distributing treats to children to attract them, though the Sages permitted it because his competitors could do the same[3].

They said, "The theft of a commoner is more severe than the theft of consecrated property, for this one precedes sin to sacrilege, etc."[4]. Workers employed by others were exempted from certain blessings to avoid neglecting their work. Even for the recital of Shema, they were only obligated to interrupt their work for the first chapter[5]. This principle applies even more so to optional matters, where every day laborer is prohibited from neglecting their employer's work. Jacob our forefather exemplified this, saying, "By day the heat consumed me, and the frost by night, and my sleep fled from my eyes"[7].

The principle is: one hired by another for any work has all their hours sold for that day, as they said, "Hiring is a sale for its day"[8]. Anything taken from these hours for personal benefit is outright theft. If not forgiven, it remains unforgiven, as our Rabbis said, "For transgressions between man and his fellow, Yom Kippur does not atone until he appeases his fellow"[9].

Moreover, even if one performed a mitzvah during work time, it's not considered a mitzvah but a transgression, for a transgression is not a mitzvah. Scripture writes, "For I the Lord love justice, I hate robbery in a burnt offering"[10]. They said, "If one stole wheat, ground it, baked it and recited a blessing, this one does not bless but rather blasphemes"[11]. About such cases, it's said, "Woe to this one whose advocate becomes his accuser"[12].

As they said, may their memory be blessed, regarding the matter of a stolen lulav [13]. Theft of an object is theft, and theft of time is theft. Just as one who steals an object and performs a mitzvah with it - his advocate becomes his accuser, so too one who steals time and performs a mitzvah with it - his advocate becomes his accuser. The Holy One, Blessed be He, desires faithfulness, as it says, "The Lord preserves the faithful"[14], "Open the gates, that the righteous nation that keeps faithfulness may enter"[15], "My eyes are upon the faithful of the land, that they may dwell with me"[16], "O Lord, do not Your eyes look for faithfulness?"[17]

Even Job testified about himself and said, "If my step has turned from the way, and my heart has gone after my eyes, and if any spot has clung to my hands" [18].
Consider the beauty of this metaphor. Job compares unconcealed theft to something clinging to a person's hand; even if one doesn't initially take it, it ultimately ends up in their possession. Similarly, even if a person doesn't actively steal, it's difficult for their hands to be completely clean of it. In truth, this stems from the eyes leading the heart to seek justifications for what appears desirable, rather than the heart controlling the eyes to avoid finding others' possessions appealing. Job affirms that he didn't do this; his heart didn't follow his eyes, so nothing clung to his hands.

Regarding price fraud (ona'ah), it's easy for a person to be enticed when it appears proper to make merchandise attractive and profit through their labor. However, without careful examination, one may transgress the sin of ona'ah, about which we were warned, "You shall not wrong one another"[21]. They said, "Even to deceive a gentile is forbidden"[22]. Scripture states, "The remnant of Israel shall not do iniquity, nor speak lies, nor shall a deceitful tongue be found in their mouth"[23].

They further said, "One may not polish utensils to make them appear new. One may not mix produce with produce, even new with new, even a seah for a dinar. And even if it's worth a dinar and a third, one may not mix and sell them for a seah per dinar. Anyone who does these things, anyone who acts dishonestly is called by five names: unjust, hated, detested, banned, an abomination"[24].

The severity of theft is emphasized even for small amounts: "Anyone who steals from his fellow even the value of a perutah, it is as if he takes his life from him"[25]. They further said, "Rain is withheld only because of the sin of theft"[26], and "A basket full of sins - who accuses at the head of them all? Theft"[27]. The generation of the flood had their decree sealed only because of theft[28].

If you ask, "How is it possible not to strive in our business dealings to appease our fellow about the purchase and its value?" Regarding business dealings, there's a distinction between showing true goodness and beauty of an object (which is good) and concealing defects (which is forbidden). This is a major principle in business faithfulness.

Regarding measures, it is explicitly written, "Everyone who does these is an abomination to the Lord your God"[29]. They said, "The punishment for measures is more severe than the punishment for sexual immorality, etc."[30]. They said, "The wholesaler cleans his measures once every thirty days"[31]. Why? So they won't be deficient without his knowledge, leading to punishment

The sin of usury is particularly severe, likened to denying the God of Israel[32]. They said on the verse "He lends at usury and takes increase. Shall he then live? He shall not live"[33], that he will not live in the resurrection of the dead, for he and his dust are detested in the eyes of the Lord.

The desire for money brings many stumbling blocks. To be truly clean of them requires great analysis and examination. If one is clean of it, they've reached a great level, for many act piously in other areas but struggle with ill-gotten gain. As Zophar the Naamathite said to Job, "If iniquity is in your hand, put it far away, and do not let wickedness dwell in your tents. Then you will lift up your face without blemish, and you will be steadfast and will not fear"[34]. I have spoken until now of the details of one commandment of the commandments, and like these details and distinctions, there are certainly found in every single commandment. However, I only mention those in which most people commonly stumble

Regarding sexual immorality, which is second to theft in severity, they said, "Most of them with theft and a minority of them with sexual immorality"[35]. To be completely cleansed of this sin is no small task.one who wants to be completely cleansed also faces a significant task. Not only is the act itself prohibited, but anything close to it. The verse states, "None of you shall approach to uncover nakedness"[36]. They said, "The Holy One, Blessed be He, said: Do not say, since it's forbidden for me to have relations with a woman, I will hold her and there's no sin, I will embrace her and there's no sin, or I will kiss her and there's no sin. Just as a Nazirite who vowed not to drink wine is forbidden to eat anything from the grapevine, so too a woman who isn't yours - it's forbidden to touch her at all. Anyone who touches a woman who isn't his brings death upon himself, etc."[37].

This teaching compares the prohibition to that of a Nazirite, showing how the Torah taught the Sages to create fences around the Torah. They learned from the Nazirite to forbid anything similar to the main prohibition. This principle applies to all commandments, forbidding anything close to what's explicitly prohibited. In matters of sexual immorality, they forbade anything related to fornication, whether in action, sight, speech, hearing, or even thought.

Regarding sight, they said, "'Hand to hand, the evil man shall not be cleansed' (Proverbs 11:21) - anyone who gives money from his hand to hers to gaze at her will not be cleansed of the judgment of Gehinnom"[38]. They further said, "Why did the

Israelites of that generation need atonement? Because they fed their eyes on sexual immorality, etc."[39] Rav Sheshet said, "Anyone who looks at a woman's little finger is considered as if he is looking at her nudity"[40]. They also said, "A man should not gaze at a beautiful woman, even if she is unmarried, and at a married woman even if she is ugly"[41]. Regarding speaking with women, we have explicitly learned, "Anyone who engages in excessive conversation with a woman causes evil to himself"[42]. Concerning hearing, they said, "A woman's voice is nakedness"[43].

Furthermore, regarding the promiscuity of mouth and ear - speaking or listening to promiscuous matters - they have strongly warned, "'There shall not be seen among you anything unseemly' 'Unseemly' refers to obscene talk"[44]. They said, "For the sin of obscene talk, new troubles arise and the young men, the enemies of Israel, die"[45]. They added, "Anyone who speaks obscenely Gehinnom is made deeper for him"[46]. They further stated, "Everyone knows why a bride enters the bridal chamber, but anyone who speaks obscenely, etc. even if a seventy-year positive decree has been sealed for him, it is reversed for evil"[47]. They also said, "Even light conversation between a man and his wife is told to a person at the time of judgment"[48]. Regarding wicked listening, they said, "Even one who hears and is silent, as it says, 'He who angers God will fall there'"[49]. These teachings show that all senses must be kept clean from promiscuity and anything related to it.

Concerning thought, we learned at the beginning of our baraita, "'And you shall guard yourself from every evil thing' that a man should not think impure thoughts by day, etc."[50] They further said, "Impure thoughts are worse than the sin itself"[51]. Scripture explicitly states, "Evil thoughts are an abomination to the Lord"[52].

We have now addressed two categories of severe sins that people are prone to stumble in due to their many branches and the strong inclination of the human heart to desire them.

The third level after theft and sexual sins in terms of desire is the prohibition of forbidden foods. This includes non-kosher foods, their mixtures, meat and milk, food cooked by gentiles, vessels used by gentiles, and wine of gentiles. Being meticulous in all of these requires great care and fortitude. They said, "If you contaminate yourselves through them, you will end up becoming contaminated through them"[53], meaning forbidden foods introduce contamination into a person's heart and soul until the sanctity of God is removed and distanced from him.

This is also what they said in the Talmud on the verse, "Lest you become contaminated through them" — read it not as "and you will become contaminated" but as "and you will become dulled," for sin dulls a person's heart[54], removing true knowledge and the spirit of intellect that God grants to the pious. As Scripture says, "For the Lord grants wisdom"[55]. One is then left as an animal, physical, immersed in the crassness of this world. Forbidden foods are worse than all other prohibitions in this regard, as they literally enter the body and become part of one's flesh.

Scripture states, "To distinguish between the contaminated and the pure"[56], teaching us that even non-kosher parts within kosher species are included in impurity. Our Sages explained, "It is unnecessary to state[to distinguish] between a donkey and a cow. Why then does it say 'between the contaminated and the pure'? Between what is contaminated for you and what is pure for you, between[an animal] whose windpipe was mostly severed and one whose windpipe was half severed. And what is the difference between mostly and half? A hairsbreadth"[57]. This shows how wondrous is the power of a mitzvah, that a hairsbreadth distinguishes between actual impurity and purity.

One who is sensible should consider forbidden foods like poisonous substances. Just as one wouldn't be lenient with even the slightest doubt of poison in their food, so too should they be stringent with forbidden foods, which are poison to the heart and soul. As it is said, "And put a knife to your throat if you are a man given to appetite"[58].

Let us now discuss societal sins arising from human association, such as verbal deception, embarrassing others, misleading with advice, gossip, hatred, revenge, vows, falsehood, and desecration of God's name. These are difficult to be cautious with due to their many intricate branches.

Verbal deception includes speaking to one's fellow privately in a way that will embarrass them, or saying something embarrassing about them in front of others, or doing an action that will cause embarrassment. As they said in Perek Hazahav, "If he is a repentant, one should not say to him 'Remember your former deeds' etc."[59] They have said, "Verbal deception is worse than monetary deception"[60]. Public humiliation is especially severe, as we learned, "One who humiliates his fellow in public has no share in the World to Come"[61]. Even for the sake of a mitzvah, one must be careful not to cause embarrassment, as it says, "You shall surely rebuke your compatriot," but they added, "You might think even if his face changes[from embarrassment]? Scripture states 'and do not bear sin because of him'"[65].

Regarding giving advice, we learned in Torat Kohanim, "'Do not place a stumbling block before the blind' before one who is 'blind' in a matter. If he asks you 'Is that woman fit to marry a priest?' do not say she is fit if she is actually unfit. If he is seeking your advice, do not give him advice that is improper for him, etc."[66] Whether one has a vested interest or not, one is obligated to guide the person seeking counsel to the clear and pure truth.

The Torah perceives the ultimate intent of deceivers. We're not dealing with foolish people who give obviously bad advice, but with those skilled in evil, who offer advice that superficially seems beneficial but ultimately harms the recipient and benefits the advisor. Therefore, they said, "Lest[you say] 'good advice' etc., but the matter is entrusted to the heart etc." People often stumble in these sins daily when drawn by greed. Their severe punishment is explained in the verse, "Cursed is he who misleads a blind person on the road"[67].

The obligation of an upright person is to advise others as they would advise themselves, considering only the benefit of the advice-seeker. If they see potential harm to themselves in that advice, they should point it out if possible. If not, they should refrain from advising. They should never give advice for any purpose other than the seeker's benefit, unless the seeker's intent is evil, in which case it's a mitzvah to deceive them, as stated, "With the crooked You deal crookedly," exemplified by Hushai the Archite[68].

The severity of gossip and slander is well-known, with many branches. The Sages decreed, "and all of them[died] by the dust of slander"[69]. They explained, "What constitutes slander? For example, saying 'Where else can fire be found but in so-and-so's house?' or telling of someone's praises in front of his enemies"[70]. Anything that can lead to harm or humiliation for one's fellow, whether directly or indirectly, is included in the hateful and abominable slander before God. They said, "Anyone who speaks slander is as if he denies the fundamentals of faith"[71]. Scripture states, "Whoever slanders his neighbor in secret, him I will destroy"[72].

Hatred and vengeance are also difficult for the deceitful human heart to avoid. A person is sensitive about insults and finds revenge sweet. To abandon what nature compels, to overcome inclinations, to not hate or avenge those who aroused hatred, and to not bear a grudge requires great strength. It's easy only for angels, not for those who dwell in houses of clay. However, it's the King's decree: "You shall not hate your brother in your heart"[73], "You shall not take vengeance or bear a grudge against your countrymen"[74].

The evil inclination continually inflames the heart, seeking to leave some mark of wrongdoing. It might say, "If you want to give this man what he refused you, at least don't do it pleasantly," or "If you don't want to harm him, at least don't help him greatly." Therefore, the Torah provided a general principle: "Love your neighbor as yourself"[75] — without distinctions, schemes, or plots, literally as yourself.

Regarding vows, while most are careful not to utter God's name in vain, there are minor branches to be cautious about. They said, "Rabbi Elazar said:[Saying] 'No' is an oath and[saying] 'Yes' is an oath." Rava clarified: That's when one says "No, no" or "Yes, yes" twice[76]. They interpreted, "'Just weights' — that your 'No' should be just and your 'Yes' should be just"[77].

Falsehood is a grave malady widespread among mankind, with various levels. Some make lying their profession, fabricating falsehoods to increase gossip or appear knowledgeable. About them it's stated, "Lying lips are an abomination to the Lord"[78]. The Sages decreed, "Four groups do not receive the Divine Presence," including liars[80].

Others exaggerate in their stories, mixing lies into their narratives until it becomes second nature. These are fabricators whose words can't be believed, as the Sages said, "Such is the punishment of the liar, that even when he tells the truth, no one listens to him"[81].

There are those whose illness is milder, who aren't firmly entrenched in falsehood but aren't careful to distance themselves from it. They might speak falsely if the opportunity arises, often jokingly or without evil intent. However, this is contrary to the Creator's will and the trait of His pious ones. It's written, "The righteous hates falsehood"[83], and we're warned, "Distance yourself from a false matter"[84]. Note it doesn't say "Beware of falsehood," but "Distance yourself," emphasizing the great distancing needed.

It's stated, "The remnant of Israel shall neither commit injustice nor speak lies; neither shall deceitful speech be found in their mouths"[85]. The Sages said, "The seal of the Holy One, Blessed be He, is truth"[86]. If truth is God's chosen seal, how abominable must its opposite be before Him.

The Holy One, Blessed be He, strongly emphasized the importance of truth, saying, "Speak the truth to one another"[87]. It's written, "And in mercy a throne shall be established, and he shall sit upon it in truth"[88], and "And He said: 'Surely they are My people, children who will not deal falsely'"[89]. From this, we learn that one depends on the other. Jerusalem is called "the city of truth"[90], expressing its significance. The Sages commented on the verse "He who speaks truth in his heart," relating it to Rav Safra's integrity, to show how far the obligation of truth extends[91]. They permitted a Torah scholar to deviate in his speech only in three specific matters[92]. Truth is one of the pillars upon which the world stands (Avot 1:18). Therefore, one who speaks falsehood is as if removing the world's foundation, while one meticulous with truth upholds it.

They related a story about a place where people were so meticulous with truth that the Angel of Death had no power there. When one rabbi's wife deviated in her words, even with good intent, it allowed the Angel of Death entry until they expelled her, after which they returned to their tranquility[93]. This matter needs no further elaboration, as reason and intellect compel it.

The branches of desecration of God's name are numerous and significant. A person must be very protective of their Maker's honor, carefully examining everything they do to ensure it doesn't result in desecrating Heaven's honor. We've learned, "Whether unwitting or intentional it is a desecration of God's name"[94]. Rav said, "For example, if I were to buy meat and not pay for it immediately"[95]. Rabbi Yochanan said, "As if I were to walk four cubits without Torah and without tefillin"[96]. The point is that each person, according to their level and how they're perceived, needs to be mindful not to do anything improper for someone of their stature. The greater one's importance and wisdom, the more vigilant they should be in matters of Divine service. Any deficiency in this causes degradation to Torah study itself, which is a desecration of God's name, who gave us His holy Torah and commanded us to engage in it in order to attain through it our perfection.

Observing Sabbaths and Festivals is also an extensive matter with many laws. They said, "Great is the halachah of Shabbat"[97]. Even Rabbinic prohibitions (shevut) are fundamental. They said, "Never treat a shevut lightly, for the great men of the generation differed regarding the laying on of hands, which is a shevut"[98]. The details of these laws are explained in halachic books, and all require vigilance. What's difficult for many is refraining from work and discussing business affairs. This prohibition is explicit in the prophet's words: "And you shall honor it by not doing your own ways, nor pursuing your own affairs, nor speaking of them"[99]. Anything forbidden to do on Shabbat is also forbidden to strive for or mention verbally.

Therefore, they forbade examining one's property to see what will be needed the next day, or to walk to the edge of the Shabbat boundary in order to quickly exit the city to the bathhouse at nightfall [100]. They forbade saying "I will do such-and-such tomorrow" or "I will buy such-and-such merchandise tomorrow" [101], and anything similar.

Until now I have spoken regarding some of the mitzvot where there is a greater need to be unblemished, meaning in what people regularly stumble in. From these we can learn about all the other prohibitions, for there is no prohibition that does not have branches and details, some severe and some minor. One who wishes to be unblemished needs to be clean of them all and pure of them all. They have already said of blessed memory: "'Your teeth are like a flock of ewes' Just as a ewe is modest, so too Israel were modest and worthy in the war against Midian." Rav Huna said in the name of Rav Acha: "For not one of them put on the head tefillin before the arm tefillin. For if one had done so, Moses would not have praised them and they would not have emerged from there in peace." So they said in the Jerusalem Talmud: "One who talks between 'Yishtabach' and 'Yotzer' it is a sin in his hand and he must retract it,[as one who retracts] from those who arrange the battle lines." You see from here how far the meticulousness and true purity in deeds must reach [102].

These examples illustrate areas where greater purity is needed, particularly where people commonly stumble. From these, we can learn about all other prohibitions, as each has its branches and details, some severe and some minor. One who wishes to be unblemished needs to be clean of them all.

Just as purity is needed in deeds, it's also needed in character traits. Attaining purity in traits is often more difficult than in deeds, as nature acts more forcefully in traits. Any battle against natural inclination is fierce, as they interpreted: "Who is the mighty one? He who subdues his evil inclination"[103].

Character traits are numerous, corresponding to all human actions. so are the traits which he follows in his actions. However, just as we spoke at greater length regarding the mitzvot where greater purity is needed, namely in what people regularly stumble, so shall we speak more extensively about the principal character traits, due to our regular involvement in them. They are: pride, anger, envy and lust. All these are evil traits whose wickedness is evident and well-known, requiring no proofs, for they are evil in themselves and evil in their consequences, as they are all beyond the realm of intellect and wisdom. Each one by itself can bring a person to commit severe transgressions.

Regarding pride, Scripture warns: "And your heart grows haughty and you forget the Lord your God"[104]. About anger, they said: "Whoever gets angry consider him as if he worships idols"[105]. Regarding envy and lust, we've learned: "Envy, lust and honor-seeking drive a man from the world"[106].

However, the contemplation needed regarding them is to be saved from them and all their branches, for they are all like strange vines. Let us begin discussing them in order.

The general matter of pride is this that a person considers himself important intrinsically, and in his heart he imagines that he is praiseworthy. Now, this can stem from many different notions. For there is one who considers himself intelligent, and one who considers himself handsome, and one who considers himself honorable, and one who considers himself great, and one who considers himself wise. In general, if a person thinks that he possesses any of the good things in the world, he is immediately in danger of falling into this pit of pride.

But once a person has set in his heart that he is important and worthy of praise, the consequence emerging from this thought will not be singular, but many diverse consequences will emerge from it, and even opposites can be found among them, born of one cause yet both leading to the same end.

There will be one arrogant person who thinks in his heart that since he is worthy of praise and uniquely inscribed with virtue according to his thoughts, it is fitting for him to behave in a distinctive and honored way. Whether in his walking, sitting, rising, speech or any action, he will proceed only with great calmness, his heel beside his big toe. He will sit only supine and rise slowly like a snake. He will speak only with the dignitaries of the nation, and even among them, only in short phrases like the sayings of the teraphim. In all his movements, actions, food, drink, clothes and ways, he will behave with great weightiness as if his flesh is lead and his bones stone or sand.

Another arrogant person will think that since he is praiseworthy and virtuous, he must shake the earth and make all tremble before him, for it is unfitting that people should dare speak with him or ask anything of him. If they presume to approach him, he will frighten them with his voice and confuse them with the breath of his lips, brazenly answering them. His face will be stern at all times and hours.

Yet another arrogant person will think his heart is so great and honored that it is impossible for honor to depart from him, and he needs it not at all. To show this, he will act humbly and exaggerate his traits to demonstrate great lowliness and humility without end. His heart exalts within him, saying, "I am so high and honored that I no longer need honor. I have nothing left but to give it up, for it is already great with me."

There will be another arrogant person who wants to be greatly inscribed with his virtues and unique in his ways. It is not enough for him that the whole world praises him for the virtues he thinks he has; he wants them to further increase in praising him as the most humble of the humble. It turns out this one is proud of his humility and wants honor for what he shows himself fleeing from. Such an arrogant person will place himself under those much smaller than him or the most despised of the nation to show the ultimate humility. He will refuse all titles of greatness and elevations, his heart saying within him, "There is none as wise and humble as me in all the land."

However, even though such arrogant people seemingly show themselves to be humble, pitfalls will not fail them, for without their knowledge, their pride will be revealed like a flame coming out from among the shards. The Sages of blessed memory compared this to a house full of straw with holes, and after some days, the straw inside those holes began to come out. Everyone knew that house was full of straw; so is this matter [107]. They will not always be able to hide themselves, and their evil thoughts will be recognized from within their actions, though their ways are with flawed humility and false lowliness.

There are other arrogant individuals whose pride remains concealed in their hearts, not manifesting in action. They consider themselves great sages, believing few are as wise as them. Consequently, they disregard others' words, assuming what's difficult for them won't be easy for others. They're not concerned with opposing views, whether from earlier or later scholars, having no doubt about their own opinions. This pride turns the wise back, negates their knowledge, and removes wisdom from leaders. It's even more pronounced in students who haven't served sufficiently; as soon as their eyes are opened, they consider themselves equal to the wisest. Of all these, it's said, "Every haughty heart is an abomination to the Lord"[108]. One who seeks cleanliness must purge themselves of this, understanding that pride is essentially blindness, preventing one from seeing their flaws or recognizing their inferiority. We'll discuss this further when addressing humility, which Rabbi Pinchas placed among the last traits due to its difficulty.

Regarding anger, there's the wrathful person about whom it's said that anyone who becomes angry is as if worshipping idolatry[109]. This person rages at anything against their will, losing all reason like predatory animals. It's said of them, "He tears himself in his anger; shall the earth be abandoned for your sake?"[110]. They're likely to transgress in many ways when enraged.

Another type becomes angry less easily but is very angry when provoked. Our Sages called this "hard to anger and hard to appease"[111]. This is also bad, as great harm can come from their hand in anger, which they can't repair afterwards.

There's a less angry person who doesn't get angry easily, and even when angry, it's mild. They don't stray from reason but still harbor wrath. While farther from loss than the first types, they're not yet clean of anger. Even less than this is one who's hard to anger and whose anger doesn't destroy but is just a brief moment of displeasure. Our Sages called this "hard to anger and easy to appease"[112]. This is praiseworthy, as human nature is prone to anger. If one overcomes it quickly, they're worthy of praise. They said, "'He hangs the earth upon nothing', the world endures only for the sake of one who restrains his mouth at the time of strife"[113].

However, Hillel the Elder's trait surpasses all these, as he was no longer meticulous about anything and didn't even experience an arousal of anger[114]. This is truly being completely clean of anger. Even for matters of mitzvot, our Sages warned against anger, even for teachers with students or fathers with sons. One should discipline without anger, showing anger in face but not in heart. Solomon said, "Be not hasty in thy spirit to be angry"[115], and it's said, "For anger kills the fool"[116]. Our Sages said, "In three things a person is recognized: in his cup, in his pocket, and in his anger"[117].

Jealousy, too, is rooted in lack of knowledge and foolishness. The jealous person gains nothing and doesn't cause loss to the one they envy. It's only a loss to themselves, as it's said, "and envy slays the simple"[118]. Some are so foolish that seeing good in others upsets them to the point where even their own good things don't please them. This is what's meant by "and envy is rottenness of the bones"[119].

Others may not be so distressed but still feel some discomfort seeing someone rise to a higher level, especially if it's not a close friend. They might outwardly express joy or acknowledgment, but their heart is evil within.

This occurs with most people to some degree. Even if not actively jealous, they haven't completely cleansed themselves of it, especially regarding someone successful in their own profession. However, if they understood that a person doesn't touch what's prepared for their fellow even by a hair's breadth[121], and everything is from the Lord according to His wisdom, they would have no reason to be distressed by others' good fortune.

The prophet promised that in the future, to complete Israel's goodness, the Holy One, Blessed be He, will remove jealousy from our hearts. Then, no one will be distressed by another's success, and the successful won't need to hide due to others' envy. As it's written, "The jealousy of Ephraim shall depart, and those who harass Judah shall be cut off; Ephraim shall not be jealous of Judah"[122]. This peace and tranquility is like that of ministering angels, who all rejoice in their service, each in their place, without envy, knowing the truth and being content with their portion.

Desire and lust are siblings to jealousy, tiring man's heart until death. As our Sages said, "A person does not die with half his desire fulfilled"[123]. The main desires are for money and honor, both causing many evils.

The desire for money imprisons one in worldly concerns, burdening them with toil and business, as it's said, "He who loves money will not be satisfied with money"[124]. It distracts from worship, causing missed prayers and forgotten mitzvot due to excessive commerce. They said, "'It is not beyond the sea', refers to those who go overseas for business"[125]. We've learned, "He who increases business does not become wise"[126]. It leads to dangers, weakens strength with worry even after acquiring much, as we've learned, "He who increases property increases worry"[127]. It often causes transgressions of Torah mitzvot and even natural intellect.

The desire for honor is even greater. One might subdue their inclination for money and pleasures, but honor pushes one to not bear seeing themselves lower than others. Many have stumbled due to this. Jeroboam was exiled from the World to Come solely for honor's sake. They said, "The Holy One, Blessed be He, grabbed him and said, 'Repent and I, you, and the son of Jesse will stroll in the Garden of Eden'"[128]. When Jeroboam asked who would lead, and was told it would be Jesse's son, he refused.

Korah was lost, along with his congregation, only because of honor, as it's written, "and will you seek the priesthood also?"[129] The Sages told us this resulted from his seeing Elzaphan as a prince and wanting that position for himself.

According to our Sages, the spies gave an evil report about the land out of fear their honor would diminish upon entering, losing their princely status. Saul began to ambush David due to honor, as it's said, "And the women who were playing answered one another, and said, 'Saul has slain his thousands,'" etc. "And Saul eyed David from that day and forward"[130]. Joab killed Amasa for honor when David said, "If you will not be the commander of the army before me all the days"[131].

Honor pushes man's heart more than all other desires. Without it, man would be content with basic necessities and easy livelihood. But to avoid appearing inferior, he burdens himself endlessly. Therefore, our Rabbis said, "Jealousy, lust and honor remove a person from the world"[132]. They warned, "Do not seek greatness and do not covet honor"[133].

Many suffer hunger and humiliation, sustained by charity, refusing honorable crafts out of fear of diminished status. This foolishness leads to idleness, which brings weariness, lewdness, robbery, and major transgressions. Our Sages, guiding us in truth, said, "Love work and hate lordship"[134]. They added, "Skin carcasses in the marketplace and do not say, 'I am a great man, I am a priest'"[135], and "A person should always do work that is strange to him and not depend on others"[136].

Honor is one of man's greatest pitfalls. It's impossible to be a faithful servant to one's Maker while concerned with personal honor, as it diminishes Heaven's honor. King David said, "And I will be even more undignified than this, and will be humble in my own eyes"[137]. True honor comes only from knowing Torah. They said, "There is no honor except Torah, as it is said, 'The wise shall inherit honor'"[138]. Beyond this, honor is imagined and false, mere vanity. The pure should cleanse themselves of it completely.

While achieving this purity may seem difficult, it's not as necessary as it first appears. The thought is more challenging than the deed. When one firmly decides to possess this good trait, with a little habituation, it becomes much easier than anticipated. Experience proves this.

[1]: Chagigah 11b

[2]: Sanhedrin 81a

[3]: Bava Metzia 60a; Bava Batra 21b

[4]: Bava Batra 88b

[5]: Berachot 16a

[6]: Taanit 23a

[7]: Genesis 31:40

[8]: Bava Metzia 56b

[9]: Yoma 85b

[10]: Isaiah 61:8

[11]: Bava Kamma 94a; Sanhedrin 6b

[12]: Psalms 10:3; Jerusalem Talmud Sukkah 3:1; Vayikra Rabbah 30:6; Yalkut Shimoni, Parashat Emor, Remez 651

[13]: Jerusalem Talmud Sukkah 3:1

[14]: Psalms 31:24

[15]: Isaiah 26:2

[16]: Psalms 101:6

[17]: Jeremiah 5:3

[18]: Job 31:7

[19]: Pesachim 50b; Proverbs 10:4

[20]: Job 31:40

[21]: Leviticus 25:17

[22]: Chullin 94a

[23]: Zephaniah 3:13

[24]: Bava Metzia 60b

[25]: Bava Kamma 119a

[26]: Taanit 7b

[27]: Vayikra Rabbah 33:3; Yalkut Shimoni, Behar, Remez 660; Yalkut Shimoni, Ezekiel, Remez 345; Yalkut Shimoni, Amos, Remez 545

[28]: Sanhedrin 108a

[29]: Deuteronomy 25:16

[30]: Bava Batra 88b; Yalkut Shimoni, Ki Teitzei, Remez 938

[31]: Bava Batra 88a

[32]: Bava Metzia 71a

[33]: Shemot Rabbah 31:6; Ezekiel 18:13

[34]: Job 11:14-15

[35]: Bava Batra 165a

[36]: Leviticus 18:6

[37]: Shemot Rabbah 16:2

[38]: Berachot 61a; Eruvin 18b

[39]: Shabbat 64a; Yalkut Shimoni, Matot, Remez 786

[40]: Berachot 24a

[41]: Avodah Zarah 20a; Deuteronomy 23:10

[42]: Avot 1:5

[43]: Berachot 24a; Kiddushin 70a

[44]: Jerusalem Talmud Terumot 1:6, 1:4; Yalkut Shimoni Kedoshim Remez 603; Deuteronomy 23:15

[45]: Shabbat 33a

[46]: Shabbat 33a

[47]: Shabbat 33a

[48]: Chagigah 5b

[49]: Shabbat 33a; Proverbs 22:14

[50]: Avodah Zarah 20b; Deuteronomy 23:10

[51]: Yoma 29a

[52]: Proverbs 15:26

[53]: Sifra (Shemini 12:3); Leviticus 11:43

[54]: Yoma 39a

[55]: Proverbs 2:6

[56]: Leviticus 11:47

[57]: Sifra Shemini 10:7

[58]: Proverbs 23:2

[59]: Bava Metzia 58b

[60]: Bava Metzia 58b

[61]: Avot 3:11

[62]: Bava Metzia 59a

[63]: Bava Metzia 59a

[64]: Bava Metzia 59a

[65]: Arachin 16b

[66]: Torat Kohanim on Leviticus 19:14

[67]: Deuteronomy 27:18

[68]: Psalms 18:27

[69]: Bava Batra 165b

[70]: Arachin 15b

[71]: Arachin 15b

[72]: Psalms 101:5

[73]: Leviticus 19:17

[74]: Leviticus 19:18

[75]: Leviticus 19:18

[76]: Shevuot 36a

[77]: Bava Metzia 49a

[78]: Proverbs 12:22

[79]: Isaiah 59:3

[80]: Sotah 42a

[81]: Sanhedrin 89b

[82]: Jeremiah 9:4

[83]: Proverbs 13:5

[84]: Exodus 23:7

[85]: Zephaniah 3:13

[86]: Shabbat 55a

[87]: Zechariah 8:16

[88]: Isaiah 16:5

[89]: Isaiah 63:8

[90]: Zechariah 8:3

[91]: Makkot 24a

[92]: Bava Metzia 23b

[93]: Sanhedrin 97a

[94]: Avot 4:4

[95]: Yoma 86a

[96]: Yoma 86a

[97]: Shabbat 12a

[98]: Chagigah 16b

[99]: Isaiah 58:13

[100]: Eruvin 39a

[101]: Tur Orach Chaim 307:1

[102]: Shir HaShirim Rabbah 6:6

[103]: Avot 4:1

[104]: Deuteronomy 8:14

[105]: Shabbat 105b; Rambam's Commentary on the Mishnah, Avot 2:10; Rambam, Laws of Character Traits 2:3; Zohar I 27b

[106]: Avot 4:21

[107]: Numbers Rabbah 18:17

[108]: Proverbs 16:5

[109]: Shabbat 105b; Zohar Parshat Bereshit 27b

[110]: Job 18:4

[111]: Avot 5:11

[112]: Avot 5:11

[113]: Chullin 89a

[114]: Shabbat 31a

[115]: Ecclesiastes 7:9

[116]: Job 5:2

[117]: Eruvin 65b

[118]: Job 5:2

[119]: Proverbs 14:30

[120]: Midrash Tanchuma Metzora 7

[121]: Yoma 38b

[122]: Isaiah 11:13

[123]: Kohelet Rabbah 1:13

[124]: Ecclesiastes 5:9

[125]: Eruvin 55a

[126]: Avot 2:5

[127]: Avot 2:7

[128]: Sanhedrin 102a

[129]: Numbers 16:10

[130]: I Samuel 18:7

[131]: II Samuel 19:14

[132]: Avot 4:21

[133]: Avot 6:4

[134]: Avot 1:10

[135]: Pesachim 113a

[136]: Bava Batra 110a

[137]: II Samuel 6:22

[138]: Avot 6:3; Proverbs 3:35 - [139]: Proverbs 1:5

Chapter 12 - Acquiring cleanliness

The true means to acquire purity is constant reading of the Sages' words, whether in matters of law or ethics. Once a person has verified the obligation and need for purity, attained caution and zeal in acquiring them, and distanced themselves from what causes their loss, the main obstacle remaining is knowledge of the fine points in the mitzvot. Therefore, one absolutely needs clear knowledge of the laws to understand the branches of the mitzvot fully. Due to the common forgetfulness in these fine matters, constant reading of books explaining these details is necessary to renew their remembrance. This will certainly arouse one to fulfill them.

Similarly, regarding character traits, reading ethical sayings of the ancients or later ones is imperative. Even after determining to be among the pure and meticulous, one might still be guilty in details due to lack of knowledge. A person isn't born wise and can't know everything, but through reading, one will be aroused to what they didn't know and contemplate what they didn't initially understand. Even for matters not found in the books themselves, when one's mind is awake to the subject, they'll pay attention to all aspects and produce new insights from the source of truth. However, the corrupters of this trait are all corrupters of caution and, additionally, a lack of expertise in knowledge of laws or ethics. They've already said, "An ignoramus cannot be pious,"[1] for one who doesn't know can't do. So they said, "Great is study for it leads to action."[2]

[1] Avot 2:5

[2] Kiddushin 40b

Chapter 13 - Abstinence

Abstinence is the beginning of saintliness. You will see that all that we have explained until now is what is needed for a person to be righteous and from here onward it is for him to be saintly. It turns out that abstinence with saintliness is like caution with zeal, that this is in turning away from evil and this is in doing good. The rule of abstinence is what they said, may their memory be for a blessing, "Sanctify yourself with what is permitted to you,"[1] and this is the meaning of the word itself, abstinence, meaning, to be separated and distanced from the thing, that is, to forbid upon himself something permissible, and the intention in this is so that he will not encounter the prohibition itself.

The matter is that anything that can give birth to causing evil, even though now it does not cause it to him and all the more so that it is not actually evil, he should distance himself and withdraw from it.

Contemplate and you will see that there are three levels here: there are the prohibitions themselves, there are their fences which are the decrees and safeguards that our Sages, may their memory be for a blessing, decreed upon all Israel, and there are the distances that it is incumbent upon each and every abstainer to make to be gathered into his own and to build fences for himself, that is, to relinquish the permissible things themselves that were not forbidden to all Israel and to withdraw from them in order to be greatly distanced from evil.

If you will say from where do we have to keep adding and going with prohibitions, and behold our Sages, may their memory be for a blessing, said, "Are not the things forbidden by the Torah enough for you, that you come to forbid other things upon yourself?"[2] Behold what our Sages, may their memory be for a blessing, saw in their wisdom that it is necessary to forbid and to make a safeguard and they have already done it, and what they left as permissible is because they saw it being fitting to be permissible and not to be forbidden. Why should we now innovate decrees that they did not see fit to decree?

Furthermore, there is no limit to this matter, and it will turn out, if so, that man is desolate and tortured and does not enjoy the world at all. Our Sages, may their memory be for a blessing, said, "that a person is destined to give an account before God for everything that his eyes saw and he did not want to eat from it even though it was permissible for him and he was able,"[3] and they supported it with a verse, "And whatever my eyes desired I did not keep from them."[4]

The necessity and importance of abstinence is undeniable, as emphasized by our Sages, may their memory be for a blessing. They interpreted the phrase "You shall be holy" to mean "you shall practice abstinence."[5] Furthermore, they stated, "One who fasts is considered holy, and even more so a nazirite."[6] Regarding Hezekiah, king of Judah, they commented, "'A righteous man eats to satisfy his soul' refers to Hezekiah. It was said that he was served merely two bundles of vegetables and a litra of meat daily, causing Israelites to mock, asking 'Can this be a king?'"[7]

It is recounted that Rabbenu HaKadosh, on his deathbed, raised his ten fingers and declared, "It is known before You that I have not derived enjoyment from this world, not even with my little finger."[8] Another teaching advises, "Before one prays for Torah to permeate their being, they should pray that food and drink do not excessively enter their innards."[9] These teachings clearly demonstrate the necessity and obligation of abstinence.

However, we must reconcile these teachings with sayings that appear contradictory. The key lies in understanding that there are different types of abstinence: some we are commanded to practice, while others we are cautioned against. As Solomon, peace be upon him, said, "Be not excessively righteous."[10] Let us now explain beneficial abstinence.

Having established that worldly matters serve as trials for humanity, and considering human frailty and our inclination towards wrongdoing, it becomes evident that one should distance oneself from these matters when possible to guard against their inherent dangers.

Every worldly pleasure carries the potential for sin. For instance, while permissible food and drink are allowed, overindulgence can lead to spiritual negligence. Excessive wine consumption can lead to lewdness and other vices. Moreover, when one becomes accustomed to satiety, any lack causes great discomfort, driving one to pursue wealth through potentially unjust means, leading to further transgressions and neglect of worship, Torah study, and prayer.

Regarding the rebellious son, they said, "The Torah anticipates the end of his path."[11] Concerning matters of lewdness, they advised, "Anyone who witnesses a sotah in her disgrace should abstain from wine."[12] This demonstrates a strategy for avoiding temptation: by distancing oneself while still far from transgression, it becomes more difficult for one's inclination to draw them closer.

Even marital relations, though permissible, were regulated by the Sages to prevent excess. As our Rabbis, may their memory be for a blessing, said, "There is a small organ in a person; if he feeds it, it hungers; if he starves it, it is satiated."[13] Not only that, but even at the proper time and the appropriate occasion. They recounted that Rabbi Eliezer would uncover one handbreadth and cover two, appearing as if possessed, to avoid deriving pleasure even during permitted times.[14]

Regarding clothing and adornments, while the Torah only prohibits specific items like kilayim and mandates others like tzitzit, excessive attention to appearance can lead to arrogance and lewdness. The Sages cautioned, "When the evil inclination sees a person preoccupied with his appearance, it claims, 'This one is mine.'"

Even permissible activities like walking and speaking can lead to neglect of Torah study, evil speech, falsehood, and mockery. As it is written, "In a multitude of words, transgression is not lacking."[16]

The principle is this: since all worldly matters present significant dangers, one who distances himself from them is praiseworthy. Good abstinence involves using worldly things only as absolutely necessary. It is what Rabbi praised himself with in the saying that I mentioned, that he did not enjoy this world even with his little finger, with his being the prince of Israel and his table a table of kings by necessity for the honor of his princehood. As their saying, may their memory be for a blessing, "'Two nations are in thy womb', this is Rabbi, Antoninus and Hezekiah king of Judah whose table never lacked lettuce or cucumbers or radish neither in the days of summer nor in the days of rain."[17]

The rest of the sayings that I mentioned, all affirm and teach that a person should withdraw from anything that is worldly pleasure in order not to fall into its danger.

However, there is also harmful abstinence, practiced by those who not only refrain from non-essential worldly matters but also deprive themselves of necessities, afflicting their bodies in ways God never intended. Our Sages taught, "It is forbidden for a person to afflict himself,"[18] and regarding charity, "One who needs to take and does not is spilling blood."[19] They emphasized, "Sustain the soul I have placed in you,"[20] and "One who fasts unnecessarily is called a sinner."[21]

Hillel interpreted the verse "The merciful man does good to his own soul"[22] as referring to eating in the morning, and he would wash his face and hands in honor of his Maker, even more so than for the icons of kings. The true rule is this: one should withdraw from non-essential worldly matters but partake in what is necessary.

Withdrawing from necessities is sinful. While this principle is reliable, applying it to specific situations requires careful judgment and wisdom, as it is impossible to anticipate every scenario.

[1] Yevamot 20a

[2] Jerusalem Talmud Nedarim 9:1

[3] Jerusalem Talmud Kiddushin 4:12

[4] Ecclesiastes 2:10

[5] Sifra Kedoshim 1; Yalkut Shimoni Kedoshim 604; Leviticus 19:2

[6] Taanit 11a

[7] Pesikta d'Rav Kahana 6:2

[8] Ketubot 104a

[9] Yalkut Shimoni Torah Va'etchanan 435; see Tanna d'vei Eliyahu 26

[10] Ecclesiastes 7:16

[11] Sanhedrin 72a

[12] Sotah 2a

[13] Sanhedrin 107a; Sukkah 52b

[14] Nedarim 20b

[15] Genesis Rabbah 22:6

[16] Proverbs 10:19

[17] Avodah Zarah 11a; Genesis 25:23

[18] Taanit 22b

[19] Jerusalem Talmud Peah 8:8

[20] Taanit 22b; Genesis 2:7

[21] Taanit 11a

[22] Leviticus Rabbah 34:3; Proverbs 11:17

Chapter 14 - Aspects of Abstinence

Abstinence consists of three main parts: abstinence in pleasures, in laws, and in customs. Abstinence in pleasures, as mentioned earlier, involves taking from worldly matters only what is absolutely necessary. This includes anything pleasurable to the senses, such as food, sexual relations, clothing, leisure walks, and music, except when pleasure is a mitzvah.

Abstinence in laws means always being strict with them, considering even individual opinions in disagreements if their reasoning seems sound, even if the halacha differs. One should be strict in cases of doubt where leniency is possible, provided the strictness doesn't lead to leniency elsewhere. Our Sages explained Ezekiel's statement [1], "Behold, my soul has not been defiled" (Ezekiel 4:14), as meaning he didn't eat from an animal a sage ruled permissible, nor meat from an injured animal. While permissible by strict law, he was stringent with himself. Those practicing abstinence must distance themselves from what's unseemly, what's similar to it, and what's similar to the similar.

Mar Ukva exemplified this, saying [2], "In this matter, I am vinegar the son of wine compared to my father. If my father ate meat one day, he wouldn't eat cheese until the same time the next day. But I, in this meal I don't eat them together, but in another meal I will." The halachic ruling isn't like his father's practice, otherwise Mar Ukva wouldn't have acted differently.

His father was stricter in his abstinence, hence Mar Ukva's self-description.

Abstinence in customs involves seclusion and separation from civic society to focus on service and proper contemplation, without veering to extremes. Our Sages said [3], "A person's mind should always be mixed with other people," and [4], "A sword upon the badim and they became foolish" (Jeremiah 50:36), interpreted as "A sword upon the enemies of Torah scholars who sit alone (bad b'bad) and engage in Torah study." One should connect with good people when necessary for learning or livelihood, then seclude oneself to cleave to God and attain true service. This includes minimizing speech, avoiding idle chatter, not looking beyond one's immediate surroundings, and similar practices that become second nature.

While these three parts are presented as brief principles, they encompass many of a person's actions. As stated before, it's impossible to convey all details; they must be weighed by intellect to guide them according to the uprightness and truth of the principle.

[1]: Chullin 44b; ibid. 37b
[2]: Chullin 105a
[3]: Ketubot 17a
[4]: Makkot 10a

Chapter 15 - Acquiring abstinence

The most effective way to acquire abstinence is to contemplate the inferiority and baseness of this world's pleasures, and the great evils likely to arise from them. What inclines our nature toward these pleasures, requiring such effort to separate from them, is the enticement of the eyes drawn to the seemingly good and pleasant appearance of things. This enticement caused the first sin, as attested in Genesis 3:6, "And the woman saw that the tree was good for food and that it was a delight to the eyes, etc., and she took of its fruit and ate."[1] However, when one realizes that this good is completely false and imaginary, without permanence, and that the evil in it is real or likely to occur, they will naturally despise it. Therefore, one must teach their intellect to recognize the weakness and falsehood of these pleasures until they despise them naturally and find it easy to reject them.

The pleasure of food, being the most tangible, is a prime example. It's fleeting and perishable, lasting only as long as it's in the throat - once it descends to the intestines, its memory is lost. One will be equally satiated whether they ate luxurious foods or coarse bread. Moreover, considering the potential illnesses, heaviness after eating, and mental fog that can result, a person will certainly not desire this, as its benefit is not truly beneficial and its evil is real. All other worldly pleasures are similar - upon contemplation, one sees that even the imagined good is short-lived, while the potential evil is difficult and long-lasting. It's not fitting for any intelligent person to risk these evils for such fleeting pleasure. By consistently contemplating this truth, one gradually escapes the prison of foolishness that material desires create, and will no longer be enticed by false pleasures. They will then despise these pleasures and understand that they should only take from the world what is absolutely necessary. Just as contemplating this matter leads to acquiring abstinence, ignorance of it corrupts it. Constantly being among those who pursue honor and increase vanity can also be detrimental, as seeing such perceived greatness can arouse desire for it. Even if one doesn't succumb to their evil inclination, they're still in danger. As Solomon said, "It is better to go to the house of mourning than to go to the house of feasting."[2]

Seclusion is most precious, as it removes worldly matters from one's sight and desire from one's heart. King David praised seclusion, saying, "Oh, that I had the wings of a dove, etc. I would wander far off, I would lodge in the wilderness, Selah."[3] The prophets Elijah and Elisha also chose secluded mountain dwellings. The first pious sages followed this path, finding it most conducive to acquiring perfect abstinence, preventing their fellows' nonsense from preoccupying them with vanities. When acquiring abstinence, one should be cautious not to leap to the furthest extreme in a single moment, as this will likely fail. Instead, one should withdraw gradually - acquiring some today, adding more tomorrow, until it becomes habitual and second nature.

[1]: Genesis 3:6.

[2]: Ecclesiastes 7:2. - [3]: Psalms 55:7-8.

Chapter 16 - Purity

Purity is the refinement of the heart and thoughts. David expressed this, saying, "Create in me a pure heart, O God."[1] It means that a person should not allow the evil inclination any place in their actions; rather, all deeds should be guided by wisdom and awe, not by sin and desire. This applies even to physical and material actions. Even after practicing abstinence, taking only what's absolutely necessary from the world, one still needs to purify their heart and thoughts so that even with that little they take, their intention isn't for pleasure and desire at all. Instead, their intention should be for the good that results from that action, guided by wisdom and service. This is illustrated by the story of Rabbi Eliezer, who would uncover a handbreadth and cover two handbreadths, resembling one possessed by a demon, for he derived no pleasure at all, performing the act solely for the sake of the mitzvah and service[2]. Solomon expressed this idea, saying, "In all your ways know Him, and He will make your paths straight."[3]

Purity of thought is relevant not only to physical actions close to the evil inclination, to distance them from it, but also to good deeds close to the blessed Creator, to prevent them from becoming distant from Him and controlled by the evil inclination. This relates to the concept of "not for its own sake" often mentioned by our Sages.

Our Sages explained that there are different types of "not for its own sake." The worst is when one serves not for the sake of service at all, but to deceive people and gain honor or money. About this, they said, "It would be better for him if his afterbirth had been turned over his face."[4] The prophet referred to this, saying, "We have all become like one who is unclean, and all our righteous deeds are like a filthy garment."[5] Another type is serving to receive reward. About this, they said, "A person should always engage in Torah and mitzvot, even if not for their own sake, as through doing so not for their own sake, one comes to do so for their own sake."[6] However, one who hasn't yet reached the level of "for its own sake" is certainly far from perfection.

What requires even more contemplation and effort is the admixture of the forbidden. Sometimes a person performs a mitzvah truly for its own sake, as decreed by our Father in Heaven, but still combines it with some other motive, such as seeking praise or reward. Even if not intending to be praised, when one's heart rejoices over praise, they might put in more effort, like the story of Rabbi Chanina ben Tradyon's daughter[7].

Although this type of forbidden admixture might be nullified by its minority status, an action containing such an admixture isn't entirely pure. Just as only the finest flour, sifted through thirteen sieves, is offered upon the altar below, having been completely purified from all dross, so too it's impossible for something to rise to be accepted upon His heavenly altar, to be part of the perfect and choicest service of God, unless it's the choicest of actions, pure of any kind of dross[8]. This doesn't mean that less perfect actions are completely rejected, for God doesn't withhold reward from any creature. However, unblemished service fitting for true lovers of God is only that which is completely pure, where the motive is solely for His blessed name. King David expressed this, saying, "Whom have I in heaven? And besides You, I desire nothing on earth."[9] He also said, "Your word is very pure, therefore Your servant loves it."[10] Genuine service must be refined far more than gold and silver, as it's said regarding the Torah, "The words of the Lord are pure words, like silver refined in a furnace on the ground, purified seven times."[11]

One who truly serves God isn't content with just a little purity and doesn't accept service mixed with inappropriate motives. Only what is pure and clean is fitting. This is what it means to perform a mitzvah according to its specifications, about which our Sages said, "Anyone who performs a mitzvah according to its specifications is not given bad tidings."[12] They also said, "Perform deeds for the sake of their Maker and speak of them for their own sake."[13] For those who haven't cleaved to God with true love, this refinement of service might seem burdensome. However, the lovers of God and those who desire His service rejoice in demonstrating the faithfulness of their love before Him, exerting themselves in refinement and purification.

This purity of heart is the test by which the servants of God are assessed and differentiated in their levels. Those who can purify their hearts more are closer and more beloved by Him. David admonishes his son Solomon about this, saying, "For the Lord searches all hearts and understands all the imaginations of the thoughts."[14] Our Sages said, "The Merciful One desires the heart,"[15] emphasizing that God is not content merely with actions being deeds of mitzvot; the main thing before Him is that the heart should be pure, intending true service.

The heart, as king over all parts of the body, guides them. If it doesn't bring itself to His service, the service of the other limbs is nothing. For wherever the spirit of the heart goes, they go. Scripture states this explicitly, "My son, give your heart to me."[16]

[1]: Psalms 51:12.
[2]: Berachot 62a.
[3]: Proverbs 3:6.
[4]: Berachot 17a.
[5]: Isaiah 64:5.
[6]: Pesachim 50b.
[7]: Avodah Zarah 18b.
[8]: Menachot 76b.
[9]: Psalms 73:25.
[10]: Psalms 119:140.
[11]: Psalms 12:7.
[12]: Bava Batra 9b.
[13]: Sanhedrin 105b.
[14]: I Chronicles 28:9.
[15]: Sanhedrin 106b.
[16]: Proverbs 23:26.

Chapter 17 - Acquiring purity

Attaining purity becomes straightforward for one who has already cultivated the previously mentioned traits. By reflecting on the inferiority of worldly pleasures and their benefits, as discussed earlier[1], one comes to despise them, viewing them as mere evils and deficiencies of our coarse material nature. Once this is verified, separating from them and removing them from one's heart becomes easier. The more one delves into and recognizes the inferiority of materialism and its pleasures, the easier it becomes to purify one's thoughts and heart, refraining from turning to the evil inclination in any action, engaging in material pursuits only out of necessity. Purity of thought is divided into two parts - bodily actions and acts of service - and the contemplation needed to acquire it is similarly twofold. To purify one's thought in bodily actions, one must persistently contemplate the world's inferiority and its pleasures. To purify one's thought in acts of service, one should increase contemplation on the deception and falsehoods of honor, accustoming oneself to flee from it. During service, one will then be cleansed from seeking praise and acclaim, focusing solely on our Master, who is our praise, our ultimate good and perfection, with none besides Him. As it is written, "He is your praise and He is your God."[2]

Among the actions that guide a person to attain this trait is preparation for matters of service and commandments. One should not enter into fulfilling a commandment suddenly when the mind is unsettled. Instead, one should prepare, calmly readying the heart until entering with contemplation, reflecting on the upcoming action and before Whom it will be performed. This makes it easier to cast off external motives and establish the true, desirable intent in one's heart. The early pious ones would wait one hour before their prayer and afterwards pray, to direct their hearts to the Omnipresent [3]. They focused on preparing their hearts for prayer, pushing away foreign thoughts and filling themselves with the necessary awe and love. As it is written, "If you direct your heart and spread out your hands to Him."[4]

The factors that ruin this trait are lack of contemplation on the aforementioned matters: foolishness, inferiority of pleasures, pursuit of honor, and lack of preparation for service. The first two entice the thought and draw it to external motives, like an adulterous woman who takes strangers while under her husband. Foreign thoughts are referred to as "adultery of the heart," as it is written, "And do not stray after your heart and after your eyes after which you go astray."[5] The heart turns from the perfect outlook to which it should be attached, pursuing vanities and false imaginations instead. Lack of preparation allows the natural foolishness that comes from the aspect of matter to remain within, causing the service to reek with its stench.

[1]: See earlier discussions on the inferiority of worldly pleasures and benefits.

[2]: Deuteronomy 10:21

[3]: Berachot 30b; 32b

[4]: Job 11:13 - [5]: Numbers 15:39

Chapter 18 - Piety

The trait of piety requires great explanation, as many practices pass between people in the name of piety, yet they are but raw forms, lacking shape or repair. This stems from a lack of contemplation and true wisdom among those who possess these traits, as they have not toiled to know the way of God with clear and upright knowledge. Instead, they have acted piously and followed what occurred to them according to initial thought, without delving into matters or weighing them on the scales of wisdom.

These individuals have caused the scent of piety to reek in the eyes of the masses and the enlightened ones, leading them to believe that piety depends on vain matters or things against intellect and proper knowledge. They assume that piety solely revolves around reciting many supplications, great confessions, cries, prostrations, and strange self-afflictions. However, they fail to understand that while some of these practices may be necessary for penitents and fitting for ascetics, piety itself is not founded upon them. At best, these practices are suitable to accompany piety.

The existence of piety itself is a profound matter that requires proper understanding. It is founded upon foundations of great wisdom and perfection of deeds to their utmost, making it fitting for every wise-hearted person to pursue, as only the wise can truly attain it. The Sages said, "An ignoramus cannot be a pious one."[1]

The root of piety lies in what the Sages said, "Fortunate is a person whose toil is in Torah and brings gratification to his Maker."[2] The commandments incumbent upon all of Israel are known, and their obligation is understood insofar as it reaches. However, one who loves the Creator with true love will not seek to exempt himself with what is already publicized about the general obligation upon all of Israel. Instead, it will happen to him as it happens to a son who loves his father: if his father reveals his opinion even slightly that he desires a certain thing, the son will abundantly perform that thing and act as much as he can.

This behavior is evident in all times and at all hours between every lover and friend, between a man and his wife, between a father and his son - in short, between all whose love is truly strong. One will not say, "I was not further commanded; it is enough for me to do what I was explicitly told." Rather, from what was commanded, one will infer the commander's intent and strive to do what can be inferred will bring gratification.

The same happens to one who loves his Creator with faithful love. The revealed and publicized commandments serve as a revelation of opinion, indicating where His blessed will and desire tend. Such a person will not say, "It is enough for me to do what is stated explicitly," or "I will exempt myself with what is already incumbent upon me." On the contrary, he will say, "Since I have found and seen that His blessed will tends to this, it will guide me to abundantly perform this matter and expand it in all aspects that I can infer His blessed will desires." This is what is called "bringing gratification to one's Maker."

It follows that the principle of piety is the expansion of the fulfillment of all the commandments in all the aspects and conditions that are fitting and possible. Piety falls under the category of asceticism; however, asceticism pertains to the prohibitions while piety pertains to the positive commandments. Both involve adding to what is explicit in the Torah based on what we can infer will bring gratification before Him, blessed be He. This is the true definition of piety.

---

[1]: Avot 2:5
[2]: Berachot 17a

Chapter 19 - Parts of piety

The primary parts of piety are three: deed, manner of doing, and intent. Piety in deed is further divided into two parts: that which is between man and the Omnipresent, and that which is between man and his fellow.

The first subdivision of piety in deed between man and the Omnipresent involves fulfilling all the commandments with all their details to the best of one's ability. These are what the Sages called the auxiliary parts of the commandments, saying, "The auxiliary parts of the commandments hold back calamity"[1]. Even though the essence of the commandment is fulfilled without them and one has discharged their obligation, this applies to the masses of Israel. The pious, however, should abundantly fulfill them and not minimize them at all.

The second subdivision of piety in deed between man and his fellow involves the greatness of beneficence with which a person should always benefit creatures and not harm them, whether in body, money, or soul. In body, one should strive to assist each person as much as possible and ease their burden. As we learned, "And carries the yoke with his fellow"[2]. If some bodily harm reaches one's fellow and one can prevent or remove it, one should toil to do so.

In money, one should assist as far as one's means extend and prevent damages with all that one can. Certainly, one should distance oneself from all sorts of damages that can come about through him, whether to an individual or to the public. Even if their damage is not currently present, since it can come to that, one should remove and eliminate them. The Sages said, "Let your fellow's money be as precious to you as your own"[3].

In soul, one should strive to bring one's fellow all satisfaction that is within one's ability, whether in matters of honor or in all other matters. Any act that one knows will bring satisfaction to one's fellow if done for him is a commandment of piety to do. Certainly, one should not distress him with any sort of distress at all in whatever manner it may be. The generalization of all this is acts of kindness whose praise and our obligation in it the Sages spoke of at length. Included in this matter is the pursuit of peace, which is the general beneficence between each person and his fellow[4].

I will now provide evidence for these matters from the Sages, though they are straightforward and require no additional proof. In Perek Bnei Halr, Rabbi Zekkai's disciples asked him about the merit of his longevity. He replied: "In my days, I never changed my place within four cubits of prayer; I never gave my fellow an alias; and I never neglected the sanctification of the day (Kiddush). My elderly mother once sold her head covering to buy me wine for Kiddush"[5]. This exemplifies piety in observing commandment details, as he went beyond legal requirements to perform Kiddush, even when it required great sacrifice. Regarding his fellow's honor, he avoided using aliases, even non-derogatory ones, as Tosafot explained[6]. Similarly, Rav Huna sold his bread knife to buy wine for Kiddush.

Rabbi Elazar ben Shamua's disciples asked him, "In what merit did you live long?" He said to them: "In my days, I did not use the synagogue as a shortcut and I did not step upon the heads of the holy people" [7]. These traits pertain to honoring the synagogue and honoring people, not stepping over their gathering so as not to appear to be disgracing them. Furthermore, Rabbi Perida's disciples asked him, "In what merit did you live long?" He said to them: "In my days, no one preceded me to the study hall; I did not recite the blessing before a priest; and I did not eat of an animal whose priestly gifts were not separated from it" [8].

The Sages further said, "Rabbi Nehunia's disciples asked him, 'In what merit did you live long?' He said to them: 'In my days, I was never honored through my fellow's disgrace'" [9]. It is explained there, "Like that of Rav Huna who was carrying a spade on his shoulder and Rav Hana bar Hanilai came and took it from him. He said to him: If you are accustomed to carrying in your place, carry it. If not, to be honored through your disgrace is not acceptable to me." Here we see that even though the implication of "being honored through one's fellow's disgrace" is one who seeks to disgrace his fellow in order to increase his own honor, for the pious it is not fitting to receive honor even if his fellow comes and concedes to it if it will result in disgrace to his fellow.

Similarly, Rabbi Zeira said, "In my days, I was never exacting within my home; I never strode before one greater than I; I never had impure thoughts in filthy alleyways; I never went four cubits without Torah and without tefillin; I never slept in the study hall, neither a sound sleep nor a light sleep; I never rejoiced over my fellow's misfortune; and I never called my fellow by his nickname" [10]. These are acts of piety from all the ways we mentioned above. The Sages, may their memory be blessed, further said, "Rav Yehuda said, 'A person who wants to be pious should fulfill the matters of Berachot'" - this pertains to that which is between him and his Maker. And some say, "He should fulfill the matters of Nezikin" - this pertains to that which is between him and his fellow. And some say, "He should fulfill the matters of Avot" where matters of all the parts are included [11].

Acts of kindness are fundamental to piety, as piety itself derives from kindness (chesed). The Sages taught that the world stands on three things, including acts of kindness[12]. They considered it among the deeds that yield fruits in this world while the principal remains for the World to Come. Rabbi Simlai noted that Torah begins and ends with acts of kindness, and Rava said that mercy, modesty, and kindness are traits of Abraham's descendants [13].

Rabbi Elazar taught that acts of kindness surpass charity[14]. The Sages explained that kindness is greater than charity in three ways: it can be done with one's body, not just money; it benefits both rich and poor; and it can be done for both the living and the dead. They also taught that those who show mercy to others receive mercy from Heaven[15]. This reflects the principle of measure for measure in divine judgment. One who is merciful and performs kindness with creatures in his judgment too they will have mercy on him and forgive his iniquities with kindness for this forgiveness is the letter of the law being measure for measure to him. This is what the Sages, may their memory be blessed, said, "To whom does He forgive iniquity? To one who overlooks offense."

One who does not want to go beyond the letter of the law or perform acts of kindness should be treated according to the strict letter of the law. Consider who could stand if the Holy One, Blessed be He, were to judge them solely by the letter of the law? King David prays, "And do not enter into judgment with Your servant for no living being will be innocent before You" [16]. However, one who performs acts of kindness will receive kindness in return, and the more one gives, the more one receives. David would pray using this virtuous trait, striving to do good even to his enemies. As it is written, "And I, when they were ill, my garment was sackcloth; I afflicted my soul with fasting." And he said, "If I have repaid my ally with evil, etc" [17].

In general, one should not cause pain to any creature, including animals, and should show mercy and compassion towards them. As it says, "A righteous one knows the soul of his animal" [18]. Some maintain that causing pain to animals is biblically prohibited, while others hold that it is rabbinically prohibited. In essence, mercy and beneficence should always be present in the heart of the pious, whose constant aim should be to bring satisfaction to creatures and not cause them any pain.

The second aspect of piety lies in the manner of doing. This too encompasses two main matters, though many details fall under them. The two primary elements are fear and love, the twin pillars of true service without which it cannot be established. Fear includes submission before Him, blessed be He, shame in approaching His service, and honor given to His commandments, His blessed Name, and His Torah. Love includes joy, cleaving, and zeal. Let us explain these one by one.

The main form of fear is the fear of exaltedness - a person should think while praying or performing a commandment that they are doing so before the King of kings. This is what the tanna warned, "And when you pray know before Whom you are praying" [19].

To achieve this fear, a person should contemplate and understand three things well:
First, that they are literally standing before the Creator, blessed be His Name, and interacting with Him even though no human eye can see Him. This is the most difficult concept to truly envision in one's heart since the senses do not assist with it. However, one who possesses proper intellect can, with little contemplation and mindfulness, establish the truth of the matter in their heart - how they come and literally interact with Him, blessed be He, pleading before Him, making requests, and He, blessed be His Name, listens and heeds their words as one person speaks to another and the other listens and responds.

Once this is established in one's mind, they should contemplate His blessed exaltedness - how He is exalted and lofty above all blessing and praise, beyond all types of perfection that our thoughts can imagine and understand.

Furthermore, one needs to contemplate human lowliness and inferiority due to our corporeality and coarseness, and certainly due to the sins we have committed since our inception. In light of all these considerations, it is impossible for one's heart not to tremble and quake while uttering words before Him, blessed be He, mentioning His Name and striving to find favor before Him. This is what Scripture says, "Serve the Lord with fear and rejoice with trembling" [20]. And it is written, "God, You are very fearsome in the counsel of holy ones and feared by all surrounding You" [21].

The angels, being closer to Him, blessed be He, than corporeal humans, find it easier to imagine the praise of His greatness. Therefore, His fear is upon them more than it is upon humans. King David, peace be upon him, would praise and say, "I prostrate myself toward Your holy Sanctuary in fear of You" [22]. And it is written, "And because of My Name he was frightened" [23]. And it says, "My God, I am embarrassed and ashamed to lift my face to You, my God" [24].

However, this fear needs to intensify in the heart at first, and afterwards its effects will be seen in the body's organs, namely: heaviness of the head and prostration, lowering of the eyes, and folding of the hands like a servant before a great king. As they said in the Gemara, "Rava would tuck in his hands and pray saying 'As a servant before his master'" [25]. Having spoken until now of submission and shame, we will now discuss the matter of honor.

The Sages, may their memory be blessed, have already warned us about honoring the commandment and its preciousness. They said, "'This is my God and I will glorify Him' - beautify yourself before Him with commandments: a beautiful tzitzit, beautiful tefillin, a beautiful Torah scroll, a beautiful lulav, etc" [26]. And they said, "The beautification of a commandment should be increased up to a third. Up to here is of his own funds; from here onward is of the Holy One, Blessed be He" [27]. Their words clearly indicate that it is not enough just to perform the commandment, but one must honor and beautify it.

To address those who might try to lighten their burden by saying, "Honor is only for humans who are enticed by these vanities, but the Holy One, Blessed be He, does not care about this for He is exalted above these matters and lofty beyond them, and since the commandment is performed truthfully this is enough" - the truth is that the Master, blessed be He, is called "God of glory" [28] and we are obligated to honor Him even though He does not need our honor and our honor is not esteemed or treasured before Him. One who minimizes this where they could have increased it is but a sinner.

This is what the prophet Malachi protests about Israel in the word of the Lord, "And if you offer a blind animal for a sacrifice is there nothing wrong? Offer it if you please to your governor. Would he be pleased with you or show you favor?" [29]. The Sages, may their memory be blessed, warned us to conduct ourselves in the opposite manner in the service of God. They said regarding water that was left uncovered that one should not strain it with a strainer for the reason "If it is said to a layman to the One on High would he say 'He has nothing'? 'Offer it if you please to your governor'" [30]. Consider now what deficiency is there in water that was strained? It is already permissible to a layman. Even so, it is forbidden for the One on High because it is not a way of honor. They further said in Sifrei, "'And all your choicest vows' - that one should bring only of the choicest" [31].

We have already found regarding Cain and Abel that Abel brought of the firstborn of his flocks and of their fat, while Cain brought of the inferior fruit of the ground, as the Sages, may their memory be blessed, explained. What resulted with them? "And the Lord turned to Abel and to his offering. But to Cain and to his offering He did not turn" [32]. And it says, "And cursed is he who deceives for he has a male in his flock yet he vows and sacrifices a blemished animal to the Lord for I am a great King" [33]. The Sages, may their memory be blessed, warned us in many ways that commandments should not be contemptible to us! They said, "Anyone who holds a Torah scroll naked is buried naked" [34] - due to disgracing the commandment.

The order of bringing the first fruits should serve as an example for us to see what the beautification of commandments is. As we learned, "The ox goes before them and its horns are overlaid with gold and a crown of olive leaves is on its head" [35]. Moreover, "The wealthy bring their first fruits in baskets of silver and gold while the poor bring them in wicker baskets" [36]. Furthermore, "There are three categories of first fruits: regular first fruits, additional first fruits, and decoration of first fruits" [37]. Behold, we see explicitly how fitting it is for us to add to the body of the commandment in order to beautify it. From here we can learn for all the other commandments in the Torah.

They said, "Rava would don stockings and pray saying 'Prepare for the meeting with your God O Israel'" [38]. Moreover, our Rabbis, may their memory be blessed, said on the verse "The choicest garments of Esau her older son": Rabbi Shimon ben Gamaliel said "I served my father, etc. But Esau when he would serve his father would serve only in royal garments" [39]. Behold, if this is so for a flesh-and-blood master, all the more so for the King of kings, the Holy One, Blessed be He, it is fitting for one who stands before Him to pray to wear honorable garments and to sit before Him like one sits before a great king.

Included in this matter is honoring the Sabbaths and the festivals, for certainly whoever increases in honoring them brings gratification to their Maker. He commanded us, "And you shall honor it" [40]. Since it has been verified that honoring it is a commandment, the types of honor are many. The general principle is that any act through which importance to the Sabbath is shown, we must do. Therefore, the early Sages would engage in preparations for the Sabbath, each according to his way: Rabbi Abbahu would sit on an ivory stool and fan the fire. Rav Safra would singe the head of the animal. Rava would salt the shibbuta fish. Rav Huna would light the lamp. Rav Papa would braid the wicks. Rav Chisda would cut the beets. Rabbah and Rav Yosef would chop wood. Rav Nachman would carry items in and out. He said, "If Rabbi Ami and Rabbi Asi would chance upon me would I not carry before them?" [41] You will see Rav Nachman's analogy from which we have room to learn. He would contemplate what he himself would do according to his way for a person whose honor he desires. And that very thing he would do on the Sabbath.

Regarding this matter it is said, "A person should always be diligent in fear to know and contemplate one matter from another and to innovate strategies to bring gratification to his Maker in all possible ways to show that we recognize His great exaltedness over us" [42]. Therefore, all that is associated with Him will be greatly honored by us. Since He, blessed be He, in His great goodness, despite all our lowliness, wanted in His humility to grant us honor and entrust us with matters of His sanctity, at the very least we should honor them with all our strength and show the preciousness that they have to us.
You will see that this is the true fear which is fear of exaltedness that we mentioned, upon which the honor that approaches the endearment of love depends, as I will further write with the help of Heaven. This is not so with fear of punishment, which is not the primary one, and the virtues of these traits are not drawn from it.

[1]: Sukkah 38a; Menachot 62a
[2]: Avot 6:6
[3]: Avot 2:12
[4]: Megillah 27b
[5]: Ibid.
[6]: Ibid.
[7]: Ibid.
[8]: Ibid.
[9]: Ibid., 28a
[10]: Ibid.
[11]: Bava Kama 30a
[12]: Avot 1:2
[13]: Peah 1:1
[14]: Sukkah 49b
[15]: Shabbat 151b
[16]: Psalms 143:2
[17]: Psalms 35:13
[18]: Proverbs 12:10
[19]: Berachot 28b
[20]: Psalms 2:11
[21]: Psalms 89:8
[22]: Psalms 5:8
[23]: Malachi 2:5
[24]: Ezra 9:6
[25]: Shabbat 10a
[26]: Shabbat 133b
[27]: Bava Kama 9b
[28]: Psalms 29:3
[29]: Malachi 1:8

[30]: Berachot 50a

[31]: Sifrei (Deuteronomy Parshat Re'eh 68)

[32]: Genesis 4:4

[33]: Malachi 1:14

[34]: Soferim 3:16; Shabbat 14a; Megillah 32a

[35]: Bikkurim 3:3

[36]: Ibid.

[37]: Ibid.

[38]: Shabbat 10a

[39]: Midrash Rabbah Genesis 65:16

[40]: Isaiah 58:13

[41]: Shabbat 119a

[42]: Berachot 17a

Chapter 20 - Ladder of piety

The concept of the ladder of piety is a crucial one that requires explanation. It's important to understand that the challenge of piety lies in its subtlety and the significant influence of the evil inclination, which makes it particularly dangerous. The evil inclination has the power to make good deeds seem bad and sins appear as great mitzvot. To successfully navigate this ladder, three essential elements are required:

1. An upright heart, solely focused on pleasing the Blessed One.
2. Careful analysis and correction of one's actions in line with this goal.
3. Ultimately, placing one's trust in the Lord.

When these conditions are met, one can truly say, "Blessed is the man whose strength is in You... No good thing does He withhold from those who walk uprightly" [1].

Without any of these elements, perfection becomes unattainable, and the risk of failure increases. A lack of pure intention, negligence in self-analysis, or absence of trust in the Creator can lead to downfall. However, when these three aspects - sincere thought, analysis, and trust - are properly maintained, one can confidently walk the path of truth without harm. As Hannah prophesied, "He will guard the feet of His pious ones," and David echoed, "He does not forsake His pious ones; they are preserved forever" [2].

It's crucial to recognize that pious actions shouldn't be judged solely on their surface appearance. One must consider the potential outcomes of an action. An apparently good deed might need to be avoided if it leads to negative consequences. The story of Gedaliah, son of Ahikam, illustrates this point. His piety in refusing to judge Ishmael unfavorably or accept negative speech led him to dismiss Johanan's warning, saying, "You speak falsely of Ishmael" [3]. This decision resulted in his death and the dispersion of Israel. Scripture even attributes the subsequent deaths to Gedaliah, as it states, "all the dead bodies of the men whom he had slain by the hand of Gedaliah" [4].

Similarly, the destruction of the Second Temple was partly due to misguided piety, as seen in the incident of Bar Kamtza. Rabbi Zechariah ben Avkulas' overly cautious approach ultimately led to catastrophe. As Rabbi Yochanan stated, "The humility of Rabbi Zechariah destroyed our House, burned our Temple, and exiled us" [5].

The discernment of an action's piety extends beyond its superficial appearance, necessitating a comprehensive examination from all conceivable angles until one can truly ascertain whether engagement or abstention is preferable. The Torah mandates, "You shall surely rebuke your neighbor" [6], yet how often does one attempt to admonish transgressors at inopportune moments or locations, resulting in increased wickedness and profanation of the Divine, thus compounding their sin? In such instances, silence becomes the more pious choice. As it is said, "Just as it is a mitzvah to speak that which will be heeded, it is equally a mitzvah to refrain from speaking that which will not be heeded" [7]. While it is generally appropriate for individuals to be eager in fulfilling mitzvot, circumstances may arise where pursuit of the mitzvah leads to its degradation and the profanation, rather than glorification, of Heaven's Name. In such cases, the truly pious individual is obligated to abstain from the mitzvah rather than pursue it.

Consider the account of the Levites: "Knowing the great reward for carrying the Ark, they abandoned the Table, the Menorah, and the Altars, all rushing towards the Ark to claim the reward. This led to disputes, with one arguing 'I shall carry it here,' and another contending 'I shall carry it there.' Their frivolous behavior resulted in Divine retribution" [8].

One is obligated to observe all mitzvot in their entirety, regardless of company, without fear or shame. As it is written, "I will speak of Your testimonies before kings and not be ashamed" [9]. We are taught: "Be bold as a leopard," etc. However, this too requires discernment. While this applies to the core mitzvot where unwavering commitment is essential, there exist additional pious practices which, if performed publicly, may invite mockery and cause others to sin. As these are not absolute obligations, abstention may be more appropriate for the pious individual. This aligns with the directive, "Walk humbly with your God" [10]. Many great pious individuals have refrained from their practices in public to avoid the appearance of arrogance. The principle is: essential mitzvot must be performed regardless of mockery, while non-essential practices that incite ridicule should be avoided.

The truly pious must weigh all actions according to their consequences and associated conditions—considering time, company, subject, and place. If abstention will generate greater sanctification of Heaven's Name and Divine satisfaction than action, one must abstain. Similarly, if an seemingly positive action yields negative consequences, or a seemingly negative action produces positive outcomes, everything should be judged by its ultimate fruit. These matters are entrusted only to the discerning heart and sound intellect, for the infinite details defy complete explanation. May the Lord bestow wisdom, knowledge, and understanding from His mouth.

[1]: Psalms 84:6-12
[2]: I Samuel 2:9, Psalms 37:28
[3]: Jeremiah 40
[4]: Niddah 61a, Jeremiah 41:9
[5]: Incident of Bar Kamtza
[6]: Leviticus 19:17
[7]: Yevamot 65b
[8]: Bamidbar Rabbah 5:1
[9]: Psalms 119:46
[10]: Micah 6:8

Chapter 21 - Acquiring piety

Acquiring piety is greatly aided by frequent introspection and abundant contemplation. When one deeply considers the sublimity of the Blessed One, His ultimate perfection, and the vast distance between His greatness and our lowliness, it fills one with awe and trembling. Contemplating His great goodness towards us, His love for Israel, the closeness of the righteous to Him, and the distinction of the Torah and mitzvot ignites an intense love. This leads to a desire to cleave to Him, as one realizes that the Blessed Name is like a Father who has mercy on us as a father does for his children.

To achieve this, one must retreat to a private space and focus all their knowledge and understanding on introspection and contemplation of these truths. Diligent study and contemplation of King David's psalms, which are filled with love, fear, and all types of piety, can greatly move one to follow in his footsteps. Reading accounts of pious acts in the aggadot is also helpful, as it inspires one to emulate their admirable deeds. However, preoccupations and worries hinder piety. When the mind is overwhelmed with concerns and affairs, it cannot engage in the necessary contemplation. Without this reflection, one cannot reach piety. Even if already attained, such distractions confuse the intellect and prevent it from strengthening in fear, love, and other aspects of piety. As the sages said, "The Divine Presence does not rest amidst sadness, etc." Pleasures and delights are even more detrimental to piety, as they draw the heart away from true knowledge [11].

The Way to Spiritual Integrity

Trust in the Divine can save one from these hindrances. One must cast their burden entirely upon the Lord, knowing that it's impossible to lack what has been allotted to them. As the sages taught, "All of a person's sustenance is fixed for him from Rosh Hashanah, etc." They also said, "A person does not touch what is prepared for his companion even to the thickness of a hair." However, due to the decree "By the sweat of your brow you shall eat bread," one is obligated to make some effort for sustenance. This is like a universal tax from which there is no escape [12].

The sages interpreted, "Can one fulfill this even while sitting inactive? The verse declares: 'In all that you put your hand to do.'" But the effort itself doesn't help; rather, it's obligatory. Once the effort is made, one has fulfilled their obligation, allowing room for Heaven's blessing. Excessive diligence and effort are unnecessary. As King David wrote, "For not from the east nor from the west, etc., but God is the Judge," and King Solomon said, "Do not weary yourself to become rich; cease from your own wisdom" [13].

The true path is that of the early pious ones: they made Torah their primary occupation and work secondary, sustaining both. After doing a little work, one should trust in their Creator and not be saddened by worldly matters. This leaves the mind free and the heart prepared for true piety and perfect service.

[11]: Shabbat 30b, Pesachim 117a
[12]: Beitzah 16a, Yoma 38b, Genesis 3:19
[13]: Psalms 75:7, Proverbs 23:4

Chapter 22 - Humility

We have previously discussed the negative aspects of pride and the general merits of humility. Now, we will delve deeper into the essence of humility, which will naturally illuminate the nature of pride. The fundamental principle of humility is that a person does not consider themselves important for any reason, which is the exact opposite of pride. The results of humility are therefore contrary to those of pride. Upon examination, we find that this involves both thought and action. A person must first cultivate humility in their mind, and then behave in a humble manner. If one is not humble in mind but attempts to act humbly, they become one of the falsely humble, who are hypocrites - and there is nothing worse in the world.

Let us now explain these components. Humility in thought requires a person to contemplate and acknowledge that praise and honor are not befitting them, and even less so is elevation above others. This stems from both their inherent shortcomings and their existing qualities. Regarding shortcomings, it is evident that no person, at any level of perfection, is without numerous deficiencies - whether in their nature, family and relationships, life experiences, or actions, for "there is no righteous person on earth who does good and does not sin." All these flaws in a person leave no room for self-elevation, even if they possess many positive qualities, as these defects are sufficient to overshadow them.

Wisdom, which often leads to pride due to its inherent value and connection to the intellect, is particularly prone to this. There is no wise person who does not err or need to learn from colleagues and even students. How, then, can one be elevated in their wisdom? Even a truly great and exceptional sage, upon honest reflection, will see that there is no basis for pride or elevation. One who possesses greater knowledge than others is merely following the dictates of their nature, much like a bird that flies because it is its nature, or an ox that pulls with its strength because that is its purpose. A wise person is wise because their nature inclines them towards it. If someone who is currently not as wise had the same natural intellect, they would become equally wise. Therefore, there is nothing here to boast about or feel elevated over. Rather, if one has great wisdom, they are obligated to teach it to those who need it. As Rabban Yochanan ben Zakkai said, "If you have learned much Torah, do not boast of it, for this is why you were created" [14].

If a person is wealthy, they should be content with their portion and help those in need. If they are strong, they should assist the weak and rescue the oppressed. This can be compared to servants in a household, each assigned to a specific task. It is appropriate for each to fulfill their role according to their instructions to complete the household's work and meet its needs. There is no place for pride in this truth. This contemplation and introspection are fitting for any person with a straightforward and unobstructed intellect. When this becomes clear to them, they can be called truly humble, humble in heart and mind. This is exemplified by David, who said to Michal, "And I will be lowly in my own eyes" [15].

The sages said, "How great are the humble in spirit, for when the Temple existed, a person would offer a burnt offering - the reward of a burnt offering would be in their hand; a meal offering - the reward of a meal offering would be in their hand. But concerning one who is humble in spirit, Scripture elevates them as if they had offered all the sacrifices, as it says, 'The sacrifices of God are a broken spirit'" [16]. This praises those who are humble in heart and thought. They also said, "Not because you are more numerous than all the peoples did the Lord desire and choose you, for you are the fewest of all peoples." The Holy One, Blessed be He, said to them: "My children, I desire you because even when I bestow greatness upon you, you diminish yourselves before Me. I bestowed greatness upon Abraham, yet he said, 'I am but dust and ashes.' I bestowed greatness upon Moses and Aaron, yet they said, 'What are we?' I bestowed greatness upon David, yet he said, 'I am a worm and not a man'" [17]. All this is because a straightforward heart is not swayed by any quality it attains, knowing in truth that despite this, it does not escape its lowliness due to other unavoidable deficiencies.

Furthermore, even in the mitzvot one has fulfilled, they certainly have not reached the ultimate goal. Even if they had no other deficiencies, being flesh and blood born of woman is more than sufficient cause for lowliness and inferiority, to the extent that elevation is entirely unsuitable. Any quality they attain is solely due to the goodness of the Almighty, who wishes to favor them despite their extreme lowliness and despicability from the perspective of their nature and materiality. Therefore, they should only thank the One who favored them and continually humble themselves further. This can be compared to a poor and destitute person who receives a gift out of kindness - it is impossible for them not to feel ashamed. The more kindness they receive, the more their shame increases. So it is with any person whose eyes are open to see themselves receiving good qualities from the blessed Lord. As King David said, "How can I repay the Lord for all His goodness to me?" [18].

We have seen great pious individuals who were punished for crediting themselves despite all their piety: Concerning Nehemiah, son of Hacaliah, they said, "Why was his book not called by his name? Because he credited himself." Similarly, Hezekiah said, "Behold, for my own peace I had great bitterness," to which the Holy One, Blessed be He, responded, "And I will defend this city to save it for My own sake and for the sake of My servant David." And as they said, "Whoever relies on his own merit, the merit of others is given to him" [19]. Here we see that a person should not even credit themselves for their good deeds, much less be elevated and exalted through them.

But all this is what a person who aspires to be like Abraham, Moses, Aaron, David, and the other pious ones we mentioned should take to heart. For us, who are orphans of orphans, we do not need all this. We already have many deficiencies that require no great contemplation to recognize our lowliness. All our wisdom is considered as nothing, for the wisest among us is but one of the students of the students who were in the early generations. We must understand this correctly and truly know it, and our hearts should not boast in vain. Rather, we must recognize that our knowledge is meager and our intellect extremely weak, folly abounds in us, and error prevails. What we know is but a small fraction of a small fraction. If this is the case, it is certainly not fitting for us to be elevated at all, but to feel ashamed and humble. This is self-evident.

We have spoken until now of humility in thought, and we will now address humility in deed. It is divided into four parts: conducting oneself humbly, tolerating insults, hating authority and fleeing honor, and distributing honor to all. The first is conducting oneself humbly, which should be evident in speech, walking, standing, and all movements. In speech, they said, "A person should always speak gently with people." Scripture is full of this, "The words of the wise spoken gently are heard." One's words should be respectful, not disgraceful. As it is said, "He who despises his neighbor lacks sense," and "When a wicked man comes, contempt also comes" [20].

Regarding walking, they said, "They sent from there: Who is destined for the World to Come? The humble and the lowly who enter humbly and leave humbly. And one should not walk upright nor with great heaviness heel beside big toe but as one goes about their affairs." They also said, "Whoever walks upright, it is as if they push away the feet of the Divine

Presence." And it is written, "And the lofty shall be brought low" [21].

In standing, one's place should be among the humble and not among the exalted. This too is prevalent in Scripture, "Do not exalt yourself in the king's presence and do not stand in the place of great men." And thus they said in Vayikra Rabbah, "Distance yourself two or three places from your place and sit until they tell you 'ascend' and do not ascend so that they tell you 'descend.'" Concerning anyone who diminishes themselves, they said, "Whoever diminishes themselves for the words of Torah in this world is made great in the World to Come. And corresponding to this, they said, 'Remove the crown and take off the crown' - whoever is great in this world is small in the World to Come, and from here the opposite - whoever is small in this world, the time of their greatness is in the World to Come." And they said, "A person should always learn from the knowledge of their Creator, for behold, the Holy One, Blessed be He, left all the mountains and hills and rested His Presence on Mount Sinai, and it is because of its lowliness. And thus they said, 'to the rest of His inheritance' - to those who make themselves like remnants" [22].

The second part is tolerating insults. They explicitly said, "To whom does He forgive iniquity? To one who passes over transgression." And they also said, "Those who are insulted but do not insult, who hear their disgrace but do not respond - to them Scripture says, 'But those who love Him are like the sun when it rises in its might.'" They recounted the greatness of

Bava ben Buta's humility: "A certain Babylonian who went up to the Land of Israel married a woman. He said to her, 'Cook me two lentils,' etc., until 'Go break them on the head of Bava.' Bava ben Buta was sitting and judging a case. She went and broke the lentils on his head. He said to her, 'What have you done?' She said, 'Thus my husband commanded me.' He said, 'You have done the will of your husband. May the Almighty bring forth from you two sons like Bava ben Buta.'" Similarly, they recounted Hillel's great humility in the Tractate Shabbat: "Our Rabbis taught: A person should always be humble like Hillel, etc." And Rabbi Abbahu, after all his humility, found that he had still not reached the level of being worthy to be called humble. He said: "At first, I said, 'I am humble.' Once I saw Rabbi Abba of Acco saying one reason and his colleague saying another reason and he was not particular, I said, 'I am not humble'" [23].

Hating authority and fleeing honor is an established Mishnah: "Love work and hate lordship." They also said, "One who is arrogant in rendering a decision is foolish, wicked, and arrogant." And they said, "Whoever pursues honor, honor flees from them." They said, "'Do not go out hastily to argue.' One should never be impatient for authority. Why? 'Lest you do not know what to do in the end.' Tomorrow they will come and ask you questions. How will you answer?" Furthermore, Rabbi Menachem said in the name of Rabbi Tanchum, "Whoever accepts authority to benefit from it is only like an adulterer who benefits from the body of a woman."

Moreover, Rabbi Abbahu said, "I am called Saint (meaning the Holy One, Blessed be He). If you do not have all these qualities that I have, do not accept authority over yourselves." The disciples of Rabbi Yehoshua prove the point, for because of their poverty, they needed money and did not want to accept authority over themselves. This is what they said in the chapter Kohen Mekushah: "It is as if I am giving them dominion, etc." And they said, "Woe to the Rabbinate that buries those who possess it! And from where do we derive this? From Joseph, for because he conducted himself with dominion, he died before his brothers."

The rule is: Authority is only a great burden on the shoulders of the one who bears it. As long as a person is an individual who sits among their people, unnoticed among people, they are responsible only for themselves. Once they rise to authority and dominion, they are already responsible for all those under their hand and rule. For it is incumbent upon them to supervise them all and to lead them with knowledge and understanding and to correct their actions. And if not, "their guilt is on your head" is written. The Sages said, "If one who is worthy to be a communal leader does not accept the leadership upon themselves, they are responsible for the entire community."

Honor is nothing but vanity of vanities that causes a person to lose their mind and be distanced from their Creator, making them forget all their duties. Whoever recognizes it will surely despise and hate it, and the praises that people heap upon them will be a burden. When they see others exaggerating their praises for what is not truly in them, they are merely embarrassed and sigh, for not only do they lack those virtues, but they also receive false praises, further shaming them.

The fourth part is showing respect to every person. As we have learned, "Who is honored? One who honors others" [24]. And they further said, "From where do we learn that one who knows that their fellow is greater than them even in one thing is obligated to honor them?" [25] We also learned, "Be first in greeting every person" [26]. They said about Rabban Yochanan ben Zakkai that no one ever greeted him first, not even a non-Jew in the market [27]. In both speech and action, one is obligated to show respect to their fellows. Our Sages of blessed memory related that 24,000 students of Rabbi Akiva died because they did not treat each other with respect [28]. Just as disgrace is associated with the wicked, as the verse we mentioned states, "When a wicked man comes, disgrace comes as well," so too honor is associated with the righteous, for honor dwells with them and does not depart from them. And it says, "And before His elders is honor" [29].

We have now explained the main aspects of humility and their details in all the expanding types, according to the subjects, times, and places. Let the wise listen and increase learning. This is certainly true - humility removes many obstacles from a person's path and brings them closer to many good things. The humble person will pay little attention to worldly matters and will not envy its vanities. Moreover, the company of the humble is very pleasant and people's spirits are inevitably at ease with them. They will not become angry or quarrelsome, but everything will be calm and peaceful. Happy is the one who merits this trait. They have already said, "What wisdom has made a crown for its head, humility has made a heel for its sole," for all of wisdom cannot compare to it, and this is clear [30].

[14]: Avot 2:8
[15]: II Samuel 6:22
[16]: Psalms 51:19
[17]: Deuteronomy 7:7
[18]: Psalms 116:12
[19]: Sanhedrin 93b, Isaiah 38:17, Berachot 10b
[20]: Proverbs 11:12, Proverbs 18:3
[21]: Isaiah 10:33
[22]: Bava Metzia 85b, Yalkut Shimoni Ezekiel Remez 361, Ezekiel 21:31
[23]: Nedarim 66b, Tractate Shabbat 30b, Sotah 40a
[24]: Avot 4:1
[25]: Pesachim 113b
[26]: Avot 4:15
[27]: Berachot 17a
[28]: Yevamot 62b
[29]: Isaiah 54
[30]: Jerusalem Talmud, Shabbat 1:3

Chapter 23 - Acquiring Humility

Two elements assist in fostering humility: practice and reflection. Practice involves gradually accustoming oneself to modest conduct, such as choosing humble seating, walking at the group's rear, and donning respectable yet unassuming attire. Consistent application of these behaviors allows humility to gradually establish itself in one's heart, eventually becoming an ingrained characteristic. The human heart naturally tends towards pride and self-importance, making it difficult to completely eliminate this innate inclination. However, through deliberate external actions within one's control, one can gradually influence their internal disposition. This approach aligns with our Sages' teaching: "A person should always be shrewd in fear," suggesting that one should employ strategies to overcome natural tendencies.[1]

Reflection entails contemplating various matters. One such contemplation, as mentioned by Akavya ben Mahalalel, involves considering one's origins, destination, and ultimate accountability: "Know from where you came—from a putrid drop; where you are going—to a place of dust, worms, and maggots; and before whom you are destined to give an account—before the King of kings, the Holy One, blessed be He."[2] These considerations serve to counteract pride and nurture humility. Reflecting on one's humble beginnings and the lowliness of one's origin leaves no room for pride, but rather induces shame and disgrace. It's akin to a pig herder who becomes king; whenever he recalls his past, pride becomes impossible. Furthermore, contemplating that after all one's greatness, one will return to dust and be consumed by worms, should surely subdue pride and dispel arrogance. What value does one's greatness hold if it ends in shame and disgrace?

Moreover, one should envision standing before the great heavenly tribunal, facing the King of kings, the Holy One, blessed be He, who embodies ultimate holiness and purity, surrounded by powerful holy beings who flawlessly execute His will. In comparison, one appears wretched, inferior, and despicable due to one's actions. How could one then raise their head or speak? When questioned, "Where are your words? Where is the pride and honor you carried in your world?" what response could one offer to this rebuke? If a person vividly imagines this scenario, even momentarily, all pride will dissipate and not return.[3]

Another reflection focuses on life's vicissitudes and numerous changes. The wealthy can easily become impoverished, rulers can become servants, and the honored can become despised. If one's status can so readily change to what one now considers contemptible, how can one's heart be proud of a current state that lacks security? Various illnesses can, God forbid, afflict a person, causing them to plead for help. Numerous calamities can befall one, compelling them to seek favor from those they once scorned, merely to receive assistance. These everyday occurrences should strip away pride and clothe one in humility. Further contemplation on one's obligations to the Creator, recognizing their neglect and one's shortcomings in fulfilling them, should certainly lead to shame rather than pride, to humility rather than arrogance.[4]

Additionally, one should consistently acknowledge human intellect's weakness and its frequent errors and falsehoods. More often than not, a person errs rather than attains true knowledge. Consequently, one should always be wary of this danger, strive to learn from everyone, and consistently heed advice to avoid failure. This aligns with our Sages' teaching: "Who is wise? He who learns from every person," and as it is written, "A wise man listens to advice."[5]

Factors detrimental to humility include overindulgence in worldly pleasures, as explicitly stated in the verse: "Lest you eat and be satisfied...and your heart becomes proud."[6] The pious, therefore, found occasional self-affliction beneficial in subduing pride that stems from abundance. Our Sages noted, "A lion does not roar from a basket of straw, but from a basket of meat."[7] Chief among the factors undermining humility are ignorance and lack of true knowledge. Pride is most prevalent among the foolish. Our Sages observed, "A sign of arrogance is ignorance of the Torah."[8] They also stated, "A sign of one who knows nothing is boastfulness."[9] Furthermore, they noted, "A single coin in a bottle makes a lot of noise."[10]

Another factor detrimental to humility is association with flatterers who, seeking favor, excessively praise and exalt a person, magnifying their qualities to the extreme and attributing qualities they do not possess. Sometimes they even praise qualities opposite to what one truly possesses. The human mind, being weak and easily swayed, especially in matters it naturally inclines towards, can be profoundly affected by such praise from a trusted source. These praises can penetrate like venom, causing one to fall into the trap of pride and be shattered.[11]

For instance, Joash acted righteously throughout Jehoiada the priest's lifetime, his teacher. After Jehoiada's death, his servants began to flatter him, exalting his praises to the point of deification, and the king heeded them.[12] It's evident that most rulers and powerful individuals fall and become corrupted due to their servants' flattery.[13]

Therefore, a wise person should exercise more caution in selecting friends, advisors, and household officials than in choosing food and drink. Food and drink can only harm the body, but friends and officials can ruin one's soul, wealth, and honor. King David, peace be upon him, declared, "No one who practices deceit shall dwell in my house; no one who speaks falsely shall stand in my presence. I will look with favor on the faithful in the land, that they may dwell with me; he who walks in the way that is blameless shall minister to me."[14] It's best for a person to seek honest friends who will illuminate their blind spots and offer loving rebuke, thereby safeguarding them from all evil. What one cannot perceive in oneself, due to inability to recognize one's own faults, these friends will observe, understand, and warn about, thus providing protection. As it is said, "Victory is won through many advisors."[15]

1. Berachot 17a
2. Avot 3:1
3. Job 18:4
4. Jeremiah 31:17
5. Avot 4:1
6. Deuteronomy 8:12-14
7. Berachot 32a
8. Shabbat 33a
9. Sanhedrin 24a
10. Bava Metzia 85b
11. Bereishit Rabbah 16:3
12. Chronicles II 24
13. Psalms 101:6-7
14. Proverbs 24:6
15. Proverbs 12:15

Chapter 24 - Fear of sin

This characteristic appears after all previously mentioned positive traits, indicating its significance and the challenge in attaining it. Only those who have mastered earlier traits can achieve this one. Fear manifests in two types, which actually comprise three: the first is easily attainable, while the second is the most challenging, with its perfection being exceptional.

Fear of punishment constitutes the initial type, while fear of exaltedness forms the second type, with fear of sin being a component of the latter. We shall now elucidate their nature and distinctions. Fear of punishment, as its name implies, is the apprehension a person experiences when contemplating transgressing divine commands due to the associated consequences, whether physical or spiritual. This fear is readily cultivated because self-preservation is innate, and nothing deters a person more than the prospect of harm. This type of fear is appropriate for the unlearned and for women, whose minds are considered lighter; it is not the fear exhibited by the wise and knowledgeable.

The second type, fear of exaltedness, occurs when an individual refrains from sinning out of reverence for the Creator's honor. How can a lowly, mortal human dare to act against the will of the blessed Creator? This fear is more challenging to attain as it stems from knowledge, understanding, and contemplation of divine greatness and human insignificance. These are intellectual matters rooted in comprehension and insight. This fear is an aspect of piety, where one stands in awe and trembles before the Creator during prayer or service. It is the praiseworthy fear extolled by the pious. Moses refers to this when he speaks of fearing "this glorious and awesome name, the Lord your God"[1].

Fear of sin, which we now explain, relates to fear of exaltedness and can be considered a distinct category. Its essence lies in constant vigilance regarding one's actions, lest any trace of sin infiltrate or any act, minor or major, contradict His great honor and exaltedness.

The connection between this fear and the previously mentioned fear of exaltedness is evident. Both aim to prevent actions contrary to His great honor. However, the distinction that warrants a separate classification is that fear of exaltedness manifests during the act itself, during service, or at the moment of temptation. When praying or serving, one feels ashamed and trembles before the Creator's great honor. When faced with a recognized sin, one refrains to avoid dishonoring Him. Conversely, fear of sin is perpetual, a constant concern about stumbling or committing even a partial transgression against His honor. Hence, it is termed fear of sin, as its core is the apprehension of sin infiltrating one's actions through negligence, carelessness, or any means.

This embodies the meaning of "Happy is the man who is always afraid"[2], which our Sages interpreted[3] as referring to Torah matters. Even when no obstacle is visible, one's heart should tremble, wary of hidden pitfalls. Regarding this fear, Moses taught, "that His fear may be before you, that you sin not"[4]. This is the essence of fear: constant trepidation that never subsides, thereby preventing sin. If one does sin, it is considered coerced. Isaiah prophesied, "But to this one will I look: to him who is humble and contrite in spirit and trembles at My word"[5]. King David praised this trait, saying, "Princes persecute me without cause, but my heart stands in awe of Your words"[6].

Even exalted angels perpetually tremble before God's glory. Our Sages wisely noted[7], "A river of fire issues forth from before Him" - from the holy creatures' sweat, due to their constant fear of His exaltedness, lest they fall short in honoring Him. Divine revelations always induce trembling, shaking, and quaking, as scripture states, "The earth trembled, the heavens also dropped, at the presence of God"[8]. It further says, "Oh that You would rend the heavens, that You would come down, that the mountains might flow down at Your presence"[9]. How much more should humans, prone to error, tremble before God? As Eliphaz told Job, "What is man, that he should be pure? And he who is born of a woman, that he should be righteous? Behold, He puts no trust in His holy ones, and the heavens are not pure in His sight"[10]. It also states, "Behold, He puts no trust in His servants, and His angels He charges with error; how much more those who dwell in houses of clay"[11]. Thus, everyone should tremble, as Elihu said[12], "At this also my heart trembles and leaps out of its place. Hear attentively the thunder of His voice and the rumbling that comes from His mouth." This true fear should always characterize the pious and never depart.

This fear has dual aspects: concerning the present or future, and concerning the past. Present or future fear involves anxiety about current or impending actions, lest they be improper or tainted by sin. Past fear entails constant reflection on previous deeds, worrying about unnoticed transgressions. Baba ben Buta[13] exemplified this by offering daily conditional guilt offerings. Job would offer burnt offerings after his sons' feasts, saying, "It may be that my sons have sinned"[14]. Our Sages noted Moses and Aaron's concern about the anointing oil, as it was forbidden on human flesh[15], yet Aaron was to be anointed. They feared inadvertent transgression[16]: "Moses worried about misusing the oil. A divine voice reassured him. Yet Aaron still worried that while Moses hadn't misused it, he might have." This illustrates the pious trait of concern even when performing mitzvot, saying, "Perhaps some invalidation has mixed in."

Abraham, after rescuing Lot, worried, "Perhaps my actions weren't entirely meritorious." Our Sages expounded[17] on "Fear not, Abram"[18]. Rabbi Levi explained that Abraham feared having killed a righteous person among the troops, prompting God's reassurance. Tanna Devei Eliyahu[19] noted that "Fear not" is only said to the truly God-fearing. This exemplifies the true fear that the Sages said[20] is God's sole treasure, easily attained by Moses due to his closeness to the Creator. For others, physicality hinders this, yet every pious person should strive for it, as it's written, "Fear the Lord, you His saints"[21].

1. Deuteronomy 28:58
2. Proverbs 28:14
3. Berachot 60a
4. Exodus 20:17
5. Isaiah 66:2
6. Psalms 119:161
7. Chagigah 13b
8. Psalms 68:9
9. Isaiah 64:1
10. Job 15:14-15
11. Job 4:18-19
12. Job 37:1-2
13. Kereitot 25a
14. Job 1:5
15. Exodus 30:32
16. Horayot 12a
17. Bereishit Rabbah 44:4
18. Genesis 15:1
19. Tanna Devei Eliyahu Rabbah 23
20. Berachot 33b
21. Psalms 34:10

Chapter 25 - Acquiring fear

The path to acquiring this fear involves contemplating two truths: firstly, that His Divine Presence permeates the entire world, and secondly, that He, blessed be He, oversees everything, both significant and minor. Nothing escapes His sight, regardless of its magnitude or insignificance. Whether great or small, noble or lowly, He perceives and comprehends all without distinction. As it is written, "The whole earth is full of His glory"[1], "Do I not fill the heavens and the earth?"[2], "Who is like the Lord our God, who is enthroned on high, who looks far down on the heavens and the earth?"[3], and "Though the Lord is high, He regards the lowly, but the haughty He knows from afar"[4].

Once one realizes that they constantly stand before His Divine Presence, fear and awe will naturally arise, lest their actions fail to align with His exalted glory. This is what the Sages meant when they said, "Know what is above you: an eye that sees, an ear that hears, and all your deeds are recorded in a book"[5]. Since God's oversight encompasses everything, seeing and hearing all, certainly, all deeds leave an impression and are recorded, whether for merit or demerit. However, this concept is not easily grasped by the human mind without constant contemplation and deep observation. Being distant from our senses, the mind will not fully comprehend it without extensive reflection. Even once understood, this awareness will quickly fade if not constantly maintained. Therefore, just as continual contemplation is the path to acquiring constant fear, neglecting this contemplation is the greatest detriment to it. This neglect could stem from distractions or choice; any form of neglect undermines constant fear.

This is why the Holy One, blessed be He, commanded the king: "It shall be with him, and he shall read in it all the days of his life, that he may learn to fear the Lord his God"[6]. From this, we learn that fear is acquired only through unceasing study. Note that it says "that he may learn to fear," not "that he may fear," because this fear is not naturally attained. On the contrary, it is distant from us due to our physical senses and can only be acquired through study. Learning to fear is achieved only through constant study of Torah and its ways without interruption. This means a person must continuously contemplate and reflect on this matter, whether sitting, walking, lying down, or rising, until the truth of it becomes fixed in their mind. That is, the truth of His Divine Presence being everywhere, and that we stand before Him at every moment and every hour. Then they will truly fear Him. This is what King David prayed for, saying, "Teach me Your way, O Lord; I will walk in Your truth; unite my heart to fear Your name"[7].

[1] Isaiah 6:3
[2] Jeremiah 23:24
[3] Psalms 113:5-6
[4] Psalms 138:6
[5] Pirkei Avot 2:1
[6] Deuteronomy 17:19
[7] Psalms 86:11

Chapter 26 - Holiness

Holiness is a dual concept: it begins with human effort and culminates in divine reward. The initial phase involves personal sanctification, while the final stage is divine bestowal of holiness. This aligns with our Sages' teaching: "A person sanctifies himself a little, they sanctify him a lot; he sanctifies himself below, they sanctify him from above."[1]

The effort entails complete detachment from materiality and constant attachment to God in all circumstances. This explains why prophets are termed angels, as said of Aaron: "For the lips of a priest should guard knowledge, and people should seek instruction from his mouth; for he is the angel of the Lord of hosts."[2] Even during necessary physical activities, one's soul should maintain its elevated connection, as stated: "My soul clings to You; Your right hand upholds me."[3]

Given human limitations due to our physical nature, achieving this state independently is impossible. Hence, the culmination of holiness is a divine gift. One can strive for true knowledge and sanctify their actions, but ultimately, the Holy One guides them, bestows His holiness, and enables success. This divine assistance overcomes natural limitations, as it's written: "No good thing does He withhold from those who walk uprightly."[4]

Thus, our Sages taught: "A person sanctifies himself a little, they sanctify him a lot." One's efforts are greatly augmented by divine assistance.[5]

For one sanctified with God's holiness, even physical actions become holy. This is exemplified by the consumption of holy offerings, itself a positive commandment. Our Sages said: "The priests eat, and the owners achieve atonement."[6] This distinguishes the pure from the holy: the pure person's physical actions are merely necessary, avoiding evil but not attaining holiness. Ideally, they would avoid these actions entirely.

Conversely, the holy person, constantly attached to God and walking among true intellects in divine love and fear, is considered to walk before the Lord even in this world. They become a dwelling place, sanctuary, and altar. Our Sages said: "The patriarchs are the chariot," as the Divine Presence dwelled upon them. Their food consumption is likened to altar offerings, elevating these material things before the Divine Presence.[7]

Our Sages taught: "Anyone who brings a gift to a scholar is as if he brought first fruits."[8] And: "Let the throats of the scholars be filled with wine instead of libations."[9] This doesn't imply scholars' greed, but rather emphasizes their sanctified status, making gifts to them akin to altar offerings. Even inanimate objects used by the righteous are elevated, as illustrated by Jacob's pillow stones.[10]

In essence, holiness means such attachment to God that one never separates from Him in any action. This elevates material things more than it diminishes one's spiritual status. The mind remains fixed on God's greatness, exaltation, and holiness, seemingly connecting one to celestial beings while still earthbound. This state is unattainable solely through human effort; it requires prior acquisition of all virtues from vigilance to fear of sin. Lacking these, one remains a stranger to holiness.[11] After cultivating these attributes and striving for intense love and fear through understanding God's greatness, one gradually detaches from materiality. Every action and movement becomes an expression of true attachment until the divine spirit rests upon them, transforming them into an angelic being whose every act, even mundane, becomes a sacred service.[12]

Attaining this attribute demands extensive separation and deep contemplation of divine providence and creation's mysteries, leading to profound attachment and the ability to maintain divine focus even during earthly activities. Without this, one remains bound to materiality.[13]

Solitude and separation facilitate this achievement, allowing the soul to overcome distractions and cling to the Creator. Lack of true knowledge and excessive social interaction hinder progress, as materiality seeks its own and strengthens, trapping the soul. Through separation and solitude, one prepares for divine indwelling. With guidance and divine assistance, the soul transcends physicality, attaining holiness and ascending to higher levels. This culminates in the Holy Spirit, where understanding surpasses human limits, potentially leading to miraculous abilities like resurrection, as seen with Elijah and Elisha. This exemplifies intense attachment to God, the Source of Life. Our Sages noted: "Three keys have not been entrusted to an agent: the key to the resurrection of the dead, etc."[14] Complete attachment to God enables one to draw life itself from Him, as the Baraita concludes: "Holiness leads to the Holy Spirit, and the Holy Spirit leads to the resurrection of the dead."

Dear reader, understand that in this book I have not exhausted all the rules of piety nor said all that there is to say about this matter, for it has no end and contemplation has no limit. But I have touched upon each aspect of the Baraita upon which I based this work, which can serve as a starting point to expand contemplation in these matters since their way has been revealed and their path opened before us to walk in a straight way.. As it's said: "Let the wise hear and increase in learning, and the discerning acquire strategies."[15] Those seeking purification receive divine help. "For the Lord gives wisdom; from His mouth come knowledge and understanding,"[16] guiding each person on their unique path.

Clearly, each person's circumstances require specific guidance in piety. The path for a Torah scholar differs from that of a manual laborer or merchant. While the essence of piety - pleasing the Creator - remains constant, the means vary according to individual situations. A fully pious person might engage in constant Torah study, while another, out of necessity, pursues a humble trade. "The Lord has made everything for its purpose."[17] "In all your ways acknowledge Him, and He will make your paths straight."[18] May He mercifully enlighten us through His Torah, teach us His ways, and guide us on His paths, that we may glorify His name and bring Him pleasure. "May the glory of the Lord endure forever; may the Lord rejoice in His works."[19] "Let Israel rejoice in its Maker; let the children of Zion exult in their King."[20] Amen, amen, and amen

1. Yoma 39a
2. Malachi 2:7
3. Psalms 63:9
4. Psalms 84:12
5. Yoma 39a
6. Pesachim 59b; Yoma 68b; Yevamot 40a, 90a
7. Genesis Rabbah 82:6; Rashi on Genesis 17:22
8. Ketubot 105b
9. Yoma 71a
10. Chullin 91b
11. Numbers 18:7
12. Taanit 2a
13. Psalms 1:5
14. Taanit 2a
15. Proverbs 1:5
16. Proverbs 2:6
17. Proverbs 16:4
18. Proverbs 3:6
19. Psalms 104:31
20. Psalms 149:2

The Books of the Ramchal

The Ramchal wrote more than eighty books on Kabbalah, ethics, morality, philosophy, and more. Most of his books have been lost and today we are only aware of these books

מסילת ישרים	סוד ה' ליראיו
'דרך ה	תקט"ו תפילות
מאמר העיקרים	תיקונים חדשים
.דרך חכמה	קיצור כוונות
דרך עץ החיים	עיקרי הדינים
דרך תבונות	אגרות רמח"ל
דעת תבונות	ירים משה
ספר הכללים	ספר השירים
קל"ח פתחי חכמה	שרשי המצוות
קנאת ה' צבאות	ספרי דקדוק ומליצה
אדיר במרום	לשון לימודים
משכני עליון	ספר ההגיון
מאמר הגאולה	ספר המליצה
זוהר תנינא	ספר הדקדוק
עשרה אורות	מחזות קודש:
פנות המרכבה	מעשה שמשון
האילן הקדוש	מגדל עוז או תומת ישרים.
מאמר הוויכוח	לישרים תהילה
חוקר ומקובל	בנין עולם
מלחמת משה	פתחי חכמה ודעת
רזין גניזין	

Description of Some Books of the Ramchal

Adir Bamarom

Adir Bamarom by the Ramchal is a commentary on the section Adrah Rabah of the Zohar. which is a seminal text in the study of Kabbalah. The Ramchal aims to clarify and elaborate on the Zohar's teachings. Each section builds upon the previous one, leading the reader to a more profound understanding of kabbalistic thought and concepts.

Derech Eitz Chaim

Derech Eitz Chaim (The Way of the Tree of Life) is a profound guide to Jewish meditation and prayer. It is not divided into chapters in a modern sense but is rather a continuous discourse divided into sections that deal with various aspects of spiritual practice and prayer. The text is aimed at guiding the reader towards achieving a closer communion with the Divine through a deeper understanding and practice of the mitzvot (commandments) and prayer, with a particular focus on the kavanot (mystical intentions).

Hokhmat HaEmet

"Hokhmat HaEmet" (The Wisdom of Truth) is a work about the exploration of Kabbalistic truth and delves into the Ramchal's understanding of divine wisdom as it pertains to the nature of God, creation, and the path to spiritual enlightenment. It also contains a series of discourses on various topics within Jewish mysticism and philosophy.

Messilat Yesharim

Messilat Yesharim - The Way to Spiritual Integrity by Rabbi Moshe Chaim Luzzatto - the Ramchal, is a classic work of Jewish ethical literature. Written in the 18th century. It is a practical guide to moral and spiritual growth, rooted in the Mussar tradition. It's structured around the steps one must climb to reach spiritual perfection.

Each chapter in "Messilat Yesharim" is designed to be a stepping stone, gradually leading the reader from fundamental concepts to more advanced stages of spiritual growth and moral excellence. This work is characterized by its clarity, practicality, and depth, offering guidance that is as relevant today as it was when it was written.

Klach Pitchei Chochmah

Klach Pitchei Chochmah - 138 Openings of Wisdom is a Kabbalistic text that is complex and dense, containing deep mystical insights into the nature of the divine and the universe. The text is not structured in a typical chapter format, but rather as individual entries or "openings" that explore various aspects of Kabbalistic wisdom. These openings are concise sections, each discussing different elements of the Sefirotic system, the structure of the divine realms, and the interplay between the physical and the spiritual.

Ma'amar HaGeulah

Ma'amar HaGeulah, or "Discourse on the Redemption," is a kabbalistic exposition on the themes of exile and redemption as they pertain to both individual spiritual states and the collective destiny of the Jewish people and the world, particularly those concerning the ultimate redemption or 'Geulah.'

Migdal Oz

Migdal Oz, which translates to "Strong Tower," is another one of the Ramchal's kabbalistic works. The title itself suggests a focus on strength and fortitude in the spiritual realm, likely drawing from Proverbs 18:10, "The name of the Lord is a strong tower; the righteous run into it and are safe." It contains a series of interconnected discussions or essays on various spiritual and mystical themes and also includes intricate discussions of divine emanations and the ways in which they interact with the world and humanity.

Kinat Hashem Tzevaot

Kinat Hashem Tzevaot - "The Zeal of the Lord of Hosts." This work discusses the passionate commitment of God to His purposes and plans, particularly as it relates to the defense of His honor and the fulfillment of His will through the history of Israel and the unfolding of the cosmos. And the divine zeal as it pertains to the rectification and purification of the world, leading to the final redemption.

Sod Hageulah

Sod Hageulah - Secrets of Redemption is in line with Ramchal's kabbalistic philosophy, it likely explores the deeper spiritual dimensions of redemption (Geulah), both personal and collective. It blends profound kabbalistic insights with practical guidance, encouraging readers to live with an awareness of the redemptive process and to participate in it through spiritual growth and ethical conduct. Each section would build upon the last, forming a comprehensive picture of the Ramchal's vision of

Sefer HaKavanot

Sefer HaKavanot, which translates to "The Book of Intentions," is a mystical manual that delves into the kavanot, or specific mystical intentions and meditations, one should have during the performance of Jewish prayers and commandments (mitzvot). The Ramchal, in this text, elaborates on the profound spiritual roots of Jewish practices and how each act can be a conduit for drawing down divine influences and rectifying the various spiritual realms.

Zohar Tinyana

Zohar Tinyana, -The Second Zohar, is an extension of the themes found in the classic Zohar, written in a similar style. The Ramchal uses the form of a mystical commentary to delve deeper into the secrets of the Torah, expanding upon the spiritual and ethical teachings contained within the original Zohar.

Ma'amar HaVikuach

Ma'amar HaVikuach - The Kabbalist and the Philosopher is a philosophical work by the Ramchal. This work is structured as a dialogue between a philosopher and a Kabbalist and is intended to defend the Kabbalistic worldview against philosophical criticisms.
The Ramchal uses this dialogue to reconcile the seemingly divergent paths of rational philosophy and mystical tradition, arguing that Kabbalah provides a deeper understanding of the world that complements rather than contradicts rational thought.

The philosopher in the dialogue represents the rationalist approach, seeking to understand the world through logic and observation. In contrast, the Kabbalist represents the mystical tradition, which includes esoteric knowledge and divine revelation as sources of truth.

Da'at Tevunot

Da'at Tevunot -The Wisdom of Consciouness is one of the major works of the Ramchal. The book is structured as a dialogue between the intellect and the soul, exploring the nature of divine wisdom and justice. It addresses profound questions about God's management of the world, the purpose of creation, the role of mankind, and the process of redemption.

Samples of books of the Ramchal translated by Rav Raphael Afilalo

The Wisdom of Consciousness - Daat Tevunot
God and his Ways - Derekh Hashem
The Kabbalist and the Philosopher - Meamar Havikuach

The Wisdom of Consciousness – Daat Tevunot

To Understand the Fundamental Principles of Faith

Soul: My desire and will is to settle on some of the things about which it is said (Deuteronomy 4:39), "And you shall know this day and consider it in your heart, that the Lord, He is God," for these are among the fundamentals of our faith which every person is obligated to pursue, to the best of their ability.

Intellect: Where are you heading? The principles are thirteen - on which of them do you wish to contemplate?

Soul: All thirteen principles are validated to me without any doubt; but some are both verified and understood, while others are verified by faith but not clarified through understanding and knowledge.

Intellect: Which are verified to you, and which are clarified to you?

Soul: The existence, unity, eternity, incorporeality and immateriality of God, the creation of the world, prophecy, the prophecy of Moshe, and the Torah from heaven and its eternity - I believe and understand all these without need for further clarification. But providence, reward and punishment, the coming of the Messiah and resurrection of the dead - I believe due to religious obligation, but would like to have a reason to be at ease with them.

Intellect: What difficulties do you have with these matters?

Soul: The great causes overturning in the world that seem to show the opposite of providence, God forbid. Especially since reason cannot see the end and purpose of things, how God leads His creatures, and what is the ultimate aim; for the deeds of the blessed God have such latitude that no heart can contain them. I would like you to teach me a straight path to understand the uprightness of these matters, without turning right or left.

Intellect: There are very difficult and profound issues here, such as the righteous suffering and the wicked prospering, which have troubled even the greatest sages and prophets, including Moshe. They cannot be fully comprehended.

Soul: I will leave the incomprehensible details. But at least provide me with upright general principles, so I may have counsel and reason amidst the latitude of these matters. What my knowledge does not reach, I will accept is not for me to complete.

Intellect: It is certain that the Holy One, blessed be He, established His world on justice and upright, faithful conduct, as the faithful shepherd testified (Deuteronomy 32:4), "The Rock, His work is perfect, for all His ways are justice; a God of faithfulness and without iniquity, just and right is He."

Soul: The uprightness of this justice and depth of this perfect counsel is what I desire to hear explained clearly.

The Purpose of Man's Existence and Service

Intellect: First we must clarify the matter of human existence and the service incumbent upon man, to understand the desired purpose in all this.

Soul: This certainly requires much contemplation to understand clearly in all its parts.

Intellect: The first foundation on which the entire structure stands is that the supreme will wanted man to perfect himself and all creatures for his sake - this itself will be his merit and reward. His merit is that he engages in and labors to attain this perfection, enjoying the fruits of his own efforts. His reward is that he himself will be perfected and delight in goodness forever.

Soul: This foundation includes many angles. I await to hear what you will build upon it, so I may comprehensively discern what it includes. But first, is there a reason why the supreme will wanted this?

Intellect: The reason is simple, and depends on the answer to another question - why did the blessed Creator want to create creatures?

Soul: You answer a matter that is equal for both of us.

Intellect: What we can comprehend is that God, the ultimate good, wanted to create creatures in order to benefit them, for if there are no recipients of good, there is no beneficence. For the beneficence to be complete, He knew in His lofty wisdom that the recipients should receive it through their own efforts, becoming owners of that good without shame, unlike one who receives charity. On this they said (Jerusalem Talmud, Orlah 1:3), "He who eats that which is not his own is ashamed to look at his face."

Soul: The reason settles in my heart. Now complete your words.

Intellect: From this premise emerges a great root to contemplate - the matter of deficiency and its perfection. We need to know what the deficiency is, its consequences, the rectification by which creation is perfected, the way of doing this rectification, and its consequences.

Soul: But I think we first need to understand the perfection man will attain when he has completed his work and rested from his labor. Then we can understand in retrospect all that we have mentioned, for what man ultimately attains is what he initially lacked and needs to strive to acquire.

Intellect: You have spoken correctly. We can now understand perfection in general, not in detail, but this general knowledge will allow us to understand the deficiencies in detail, for every deficiency is the absence of that perfection.

Soul: Say what you have to say about this perfection.

Intellect: This perfection is simple from Scripture and reason; it is that man will cleave to God's holiness and enjoy the perception of His glory without any hindrance or obstruction. As it is written (Isaiah 58:14), "Then you shall delight in the Lord"; (Psalms 140:14), "The upright shall dwell in Your presence"; (Ibid. 16:11), "Fullness of joys in Your presence," and many others like these throughout the words of the prophets and writings, revealed to all nations. In the words of our Sages (Berachot 17a), "The World to Come has no eating or drinking etc., but the righteous sit with their crowns on their heads and delight in the radiance of the Divine Presence."

Reason also dictates this, for the soul is a portion of God above, and its desire is certainly to return and cleave to its source, as is the nature of every effect that yearns for its cause and has no rest until it attains this. But the nature of this cleaving and attainment we do not have the power to understand amidst our current deficiencies. From this we discern that our deficiencies are the distance and hindrance interposing between us and God, making it impossible to cleave to Him as we will after the hindrance passes. This is the deficiency we need to strive to remove from ourselves in order to acquire the perfection we mentioned.

Soul: The reason settles in my heart. Now complete your words.

Intellect: Before proceeding, we must clarify the existence of man and the service incumbent upon him, to understand the desired purpose in all this.

Soul: This matter certainly requires much contemplation to understand it clearly in all its parts.

Intellect: The foundation on which everything stands is that the supreme will wanted man to perfect himself and all that was created for his sake; this will be his merit and reward. His merit - because he is found to be engaged and laboring to attain this perfection; when he attains it - he will enjoy the fruit of his labor and his share of all his toil. His reward - for he will be the perfected one, delighting in goodness forever.

Soul: This foundation includes many facets. I am waiting to hear what you will build upon it, so I may discern in retrospect what is included. But first, is there a reason why the supreme will wanted this?

Intellect: The reason is simple; it depends on the answer to another question: why did the blessed Creator want to create creatures?

Soul: You answer a matter that is equal for both of us.

Intellect: What we can comprehend is that God, may He be blessed, is the ultimate good. It is the law of good to do good; this is what He wanted - to create creatures so that He could benefit them. For if there is no recipient of good, there is no beneficence. For the beneficence to be complete, He knew in His lofty wisdom that it is fitting for the recipients to receive it through their own effort, making them the owners of that good, not remaining with shame in receiving it, like one who receives charity. On this they said (Jerusalem Talmud, Orlah, Chapter 1, Halacha 3), "He who eats that which is not his own is ashamed to look at his face."

Soul: The reason settles in my heart. Now complete your words.

Intellect: From this premise, a great root emerges for us to contemplate: the matter of deficiency and its perfection. We need to know what deficiency is, its consequences, its rectification by which creation will be perfected, the way of doing this rectification, and its consequences.

Soul: I think we first need to understand the perfection that man will attain when he has completed his work and rested from his labor. Then we will understand in retrospect all that we have mentioned. The reason is simple and clear: what man will ultimately attain is what he lacked initially, and because he lacks it, he needs to strive and acquire it.

Intellect: You have spoken correctly. We can now understand perfection in general, not in detail, but by knowing it in general, we will understand the deficiencies in detail in retrospect, for every deficiency is the absence of that perfection.

Soul: Say what you have to say about this perfection.

Intellect: This perfection is simple from Scripture and reason; it is that man will cleave to His holiness, and enjoy the perception of His glory without any hindrance or separating force. As it is written, "Then you shall delight in the Lord"; "The upright shall abide in Your presence"; "In Your presence is fullness of joy," and many others like these, revealed in the words of the prophets and the writings. In the words of our Sages, of blessed memory, "In the World to Come, the righteous sit with their crowns on their heads and delight in the radiance of the Divine Presence."

A logical reason: the soul is a portion of God above, and its desire is to return and cleave to its source to comprehend it, as is the nature of every effect that yearns for its cause, having no rest until it attains this. But what this cleaving and comprehension will be - we do not have the power to understand as long as we are in the midst of deficiencies. From this, we discern our deficiencies, for just as perfection is this cleaving, the deficiencies are all the distance and hindrance that interposes between us and Him, making it impossible to cleave to Him as we will after the hindrance passes. This is the deficiency we need to strive to remove to acquire the perfection we mentioned.

Here we need a very fundamental premise.

Soul: What is it?

Intellect: That God, blessed be He, was certainly able to create man and all creation with ultimate perfection; it would have been fitting for it to be so, for Him being perfect in all kinds of perfection - it is fitting that His deeds should be perfect in all perfection.

But when His wisdom decreed to leave man to perfect himself, He created these creatures lacking perfection. This is as if He restrained His attribute of perfection and His great goodness from acting according to the law of His greatness in these creatures, but to make them in the disposition He wanted according to the purpose intended in His lofty thought. Here is included another knowledge, as they said, "Shaddai - that He said to His world 'enough'"; that the heavens were stretching and going until He rebuked them, as written in the Midrash. Certainly, He could have created more and greater creatures than He did; if He had wanted to create His creatures according to the proportion of the Creator, they would have had no measure, just as He and His ability have no measure.

But He created them according to the proportion of the created, measuring in them the fitting disposition for them according to what was intended. In any case, He certainly restrained, as it were, His great and infinite ability, so that it would not act in His creatures like its proportion, but according to the proportion of these creatures that are acted upon by it.

Soul: All this is certainly necessary, for it is of the faith that God, may His name be blessed, is omnipotent in all ways; it is impossible to set any limit or measure to His ability. Everything we see that was created from Him in a specific and limited measure - it will not be according to His proportion, God forbid, but according to what His will decreed to act.

Intellect: Let us establish this principle, then proceed to another fundamental premise. This principle: the Master has certainly prevented Himself, as it were, meaning that He prevented His ability in creating His creatures, not making them according to His power, but according to what He wanted and intended for them; He created them lacking so that they themselves would complete themselves, their perfection being their reward in the merit of their efforts to attain it. All this only because He wanted to bestow a complete beneficence.

Soul: Now let us hear this premise that you mentioned.

Intellect: The first premise we need to understand is where man's power is found to perfect his deficiencies, since he was created deficient. We are now entering a very great and wide sea, for we will need many great propositions before coming to complete our subject. You need to be very patient, to understand the matters in proper order, for this is the way of wisdom - to acquire knowledge one after another, until in the end everything will come to light as one complete matter, for which all those premises were needed.

Soul: Speak your words in the proper order, I am listening with all the patience and resolve required.

Intellect: First, you need to know that even though we have said that the blessed Master wanted to give perception of the essence of His perfection to His creatures, it is certainly not the will to give them perception of all His perfection which has no end, limit, or boundary; but on the contrary, only a small edge of it He wanted to reveal to them, in which will be all their delight in attaining it, as we have explained. This is very simple and desirable, for it is impossible for a consequent and created being like us to comprehend all the perfection of the Creator as it is said, "Can you by searching find out God? Can you find out the Almighty unto perfection?" It is found that all that creatures can attain will certainly not be even like a drop from the great sea of the perfection of the Creator, may He be blessed.

Soul: This is simple to all wise of heart, as it has been said, (Psalms 106:2), "Who can express the mighty acts of the Lord," etc.

Intellect: Now, when we consider all the orders of His deeds, all the great deeds He has done since placing man upon the earth, all that He has promised us to do through His holy prophets, what becomes clear to us with absolute clarity is the intensity of His unity. We see that all the other attributes of His perfection which have no end are not clarified to us at all, for we do not have the power to comprehend them. For example, we know that He is wise, but we have not comprehended the end of His wisdom; we know that He knows, but we have not comprehended His knowledge. Therefore they said, (Prayer of Elijah, Tikunei Zohar, Second Introduction), "You are wise, but not with a known wisdom, You are understanding, but not with a known understanding." Since we cannot comprehend these attributes, it follows that we are prohibited from investigating them, for about all such things it is said (Chagigah 13a in the name of Ben Sira 3:21), "You shall not seek what is too wonderful for you, you shall not investigate what is concealed from you"; so they said, (Sefer Yetzirah, Chapter 1), "If your heart runs - return to the place."

But His unity, on the contrary, is revealed and clarified to us with complete clarity. It follows that not only is it clarified to us, but we are obligated to consider this knowledge, to implant it in our hearts with complete resolve without any doubt at all. This is what Moshe our teacher, peace be upon him, commanded us from the mouth of the Almighty (Deuteronomy 4:39), "Know therefore this day, and consider it in your heart, that the Lord He is God in heaven above, and upon the earth beneath; there is none else."

The supreme mouth testifies of Himself and informs that all that is gathered from all His great causes with which He overturns in

His world, is the revelation of this complete unity; as it is said, (Deuteronomy 32:39), "See now that I, even I, am He, and there is no god with Me," this verse was said after He included the entire cycle of the wheel, which was destined and prepared to revolve in the world, all included in the words of the song of Ha'azinu, as the plain meaning of the verses proves.

He sealed the conclusion of His vision with this language, "See now that I, even I, am He," etc. In the words of the prophet Isaiah, it is clarified explicitly (Isaiah 43:10-11), "That you may know and believe Me, understand that I am He; before Me there was no God formed, neither shall any be after Me. I, even I, am the Lord, and beside Me there is no savior"; as it is written (Isaiah 44:6), "I am the first, I am the last, and beside Me there is no God"; as it is written (Isaiah 44:6-7, "That they may know from the rising of the sun, and from the west, that there is none beside Me; I am the Lord, and there is none else; I form the light, and create darkness; I make peace, and create evil; I am the Lord, that does all these things." "That they may know," "that you may know and understand" it is written, implying that He wants us to know with knowledge and understanding.

The ultimate of all the success that He promises to Israel is the clarification of His unity to the eyes of all. This matter is mentioned countless times in the words of the prophets, peace be upon them (Isaiah 2:11), "And the Lord alone shall be exalted in that day"; Zechariah 14:9), "And the Lord shall be king... in that day shall the Lord be One, and His name one"; (Zephaniah 3:9), "For then will I turn to the peoples a pure language, that they may all call upon the name of the Lord, to serve Him with one consent." In the end, this is our testimony every day continually (Deuteronomy 6:4), "Hear, O Israel: The Lord our God, the Lord is one."

It is found that all that is truly clarified to us from the intensity of His infinite perfection is only His complete unity. When we look with a contemplative gaze at all the deeds that have been done under the heavens, we see one course that revolves and goes, its rest being only the revelation of this truth. Now we need to understand this unity, what is desired in it, as the verse commanded us, (Deuteronomy 4:39), "and consider it in your heart that the Lord He is God," etc., implying that it requires the resolve of the mind and proper counsel in this matter. I have already said, this is a great and wide sea, in which we have to sail to our heart's content.

God and His Ways - Derekh Hashem

Introduction by the Ramchal

The sublime advantage of comprehending reality through grasping the precise configuration and interrelation of its constituent parts, rather than viewing it as an undifferentiated whole, is akin to the difference between observing an orderly garden beautifully arranged into beds, paths and rows, versus seeing a chaotic thicket or tangled forest. For though one may conceptualize many parts whose authentic connections and positioning within the integrated structure remains unknown, this leaves the intellect that yearns for true understanding burdened without satisfaction. Each element pictured in isolation excites curiosity about its completion within the whole, yet its deficient portrayal precludes this, thus troubling the mind and paining it with unquenched longing and unremitting confusion.

In dramatic contrast, one who properly discerns the nature of each part according to its various aspects beholds the subject unveiled before him in its fullness. The intellect then delights, following wherever interest leads within the beauty of its composition, as coherent comprehension is attained. For integral to properly understanding any topic is recognizing its essence and distinguishing parameters.

Thus, one must firstly determine the fundamental categorization and station of each element within the framework of reality. The primordial classifications are: whole or part; generality or particular; cause or effect; conveyer or addon. Correspondingly, initial analysis of any subject must establish whether it is a complete entity or constituent component; a universal principle or specific detail; an originating cause or resultant outcome; an underlying substrate or accrued attribute.

Profoundly, the precise aspects warranting examination stem from its innate properties and role. If part, one must identify the whole it helps comprise. If particular, its belonging generality is sought. Effects are traced to causes, and causes to antecedents. Adjuncts are scrutinized in light of their bearer. Additionally, the adjunct's nature is examined - whether preceding, following or concomitant; whether essential or happenstantial; potential or extant; etc. For absent such methodical distinctions, no well-formed conceptualization is possible.

Most crucially, the absolute or delimited nature of each matter must be determined, with clear recognition of any relevant parameters. For misconstruing an entity by ascribing inappropriate qualities or considering it out of context engenders misconception. Though particulars may be enumerable only to an infinite intellect, one should strive to understand essential general principles. Since generalities intrinsically contain innumerable details, properly grasping a key universal concept enlightens one to the truth of myriads of particulars subsumed within it, suddenly recognizing each one that becomes known through its self-evident belonging to that broader reality. As our sages advise, "One should always have matters of Torah as generalities, not particulars."

Yet general principles must also be properly understood in their full scope and aspects. No detail is truly negligible or unworthy of concern, for nothing exists devoid of consequence at some level. While some specifics may be irrelevant in certain contexts, their impact elsewhere remains significant, given the all-encompassing nature of each general truth that must suffice in every respect. Careful attention and precise tracing of the progression through which each detail flows from prior elements and coalesces into subsequent effects is therefore imperative, that one may gain true wisdom and enlightenment.

Accordingly, dear reader, I have composed this work to elucidate the foundations of faith and service definitively, in a clear systematic manner facilitating authentic comprehension of these pivotal principles in all their aspects, saved from confusion. Herein their roots and branches are bared, interrelations explained, such that they take root and become absorbed within your heart and soul, for the perfection of your mind and being. From this basis, attainment of the knowledge of God throughout Torah, and comprehension of all its hidden treasures, will readily unfold through divine blessing.

I have diligently endeavored to present the ideas in a compelling progression, and language optimally expressive, to impart an accurate picture of these essential ideas I wish to share. Therefore, gentle friend, I ask that you likewise examine this work carefully, hold fast to its guidance, and do not overlook any detail, that no indispensable matter elude you. But delve thoroughly into its words to grasp each concept in its full depth of meaning, that its truths permeate your consciousness, and you find the tranquil clarity for which your soul surely yearns.

This text's title, Derech Hashem, meaning "God and His Ways or The Way of God," reflects its focus: the path of divine truth revealed by the prophets and in the Torah, through which He shapes reality and guides humankind. Correspondingly, this work unfolds in four sections: first, the foundations of existence; second, God's providence; third, prophecy; and fourth, proper service. May each word awaken within you vision and understanding, that you may walk amidst the wonders of His wisdom and ways.

Therefore my brother, who genuinely seek closeness with Hashem, take this as your guide, that God be with you. For He bestows discerning eyes and attentive ears to glimpse the hidden marvels embedded in Torah's every layer of meaning.

On the Existence of God

Every Jew must believe and know that there exists a first Being, eternal and everlasting, who brought into existence and continues to bring into existence all that exists, and He is God, blessed be He.

It must also be known that the truth of this Being, blessed be He, is completely beyond grasp by anything other than Him. Only this is known about Him: that He is a perfect Being in all manners of perfection, and absolutely no deficiency exists in Him. These matters we know through tradition from the Patriarchs and Prophets. All of Israel attained them at the event of Mount Sinai and stood firmly upon their truth. They taught them to their children throughout the generations, as Moses our teacher commanded by the mouth of the Almighty—"Lest you forget the things your eyes beheld etc. You shall make them known to your children and grandchildren." [1]

However, all these matters are also proven true by intellectual investigation through conclusive proofs. It will be shown to be necessary that they are so, from the existent beings and their conceptions that we see with our eyes, according to the science of nature, geometry, astronomy, and other sciences. From them will be taken true premises which will yield a demonstration of these true matters. However, we will not elaborate on this now, but only present the premises for their truth. Then, we will arrange the matters clearly, according to the tradition in our possession and what is well known throughout our nation.

It must be known that the existence of this Being, blessed be He, is a necessary existence, that it is completely impossible for Him not to exist.

It must also be known that His existence does not depend on anything else whatsoever; rather, His existence is necessary of itself.

Similarly, it must be known that the existence of God is a simple, unique existence without any composition or multiplicity. All perfection exists within Him in a simple manner. Meaning that as it is for the soul, where are found many varied powers, each of which has its own definition. For example, memory is one power, desire is another power, as is imagination, and none of these enters into the definition of the other at all. The faculty of memory is one definition, and desire is another, and desire does not enter into the definition of memory, nor memory into the definition of desire, and so on for all of them.

However, God, blessed be He, does not possess varied powers, even though in truth there are within Him varied matters—for He indeed desires. He is wise, powerful, and perfect with all perfection. However, the truth of His existence is a singular matter that truly includes within its truth and definition— meaning the truth of its matter—that all perfection is necessarily inherent within it and all deficiencies are necessarily absent from it.

It turns out that all perfection exists within Him not as something added onto His essence and the truth of His matter, but rather due to the truth of His matter itself, which includes all perfection within its truth, for it is impossible for that matter to exist without all perfection inherently.

Behold, in truth, this approach is extremely beyond our grasp and conception. We have virtually no way to explain it nor words to expound it. Our conception and imagination encompass only compound matters bounded by the nature created from Him, for that is what our senses sense and bring the conception of to the intellect.

But in creations, the matters are many and separate. However, we have already prefaced that the truth of His existence is beyond grasp. Nothing can be inferred about the Creator from what is observed in creations, for their matters and existence are not at all equivalent such that we could deduce from one about the other. But this too is from the matters known through tradition, as stated, and proven true through investigation of nature itself, in its laws and dynamics.

For it is certainly impossible that a singular Being found, devoid of all nature's laws, boundaries, and limitations; devoid of any absence or deficiency; of any multiplicity or composition; of any relativity or finite measure; and of any of the attributes of creations. He would be the true cause for all existents and all generated within them. For without this, the existence of these beings we observe and their continuity would have been impossible.

It also must be known that this Being, blessed be He, must necessarily be one and no more. Meaning, it is impossible for multiple existents whose existence is necessary of themselves to exist, but only a singular one must exist with this kind of necessary perfect existence. If any other existents are found, they will only exist because He wills them into existence through His will. All existents would depend on Him and not exist of themselves.

It turns out that these foundational cognitions are six, and they are: the truth of His existence, His perfection, the necessity of His existence, His independence, His simplicity, and His unity.

The Purpose of Creation

The purpose of creation is the bestowal of goodness from His own abundance, blessed be He, unto something other than Himself. When you consider this, you realize that He alone, blessed be He, embodies true perfection, completely free from any deficiency. There is no other form of perfection that can compare to His.

Consequently, any form of perfection separate from His is not genuine perfection. It is only termed as perfection in comparison to something that has more flaws. However, absolute perfection is nothing but His own, blessed be He. Thus, His desire to bestow goodness upon another cannot be fulfilled by giving just some goodness; He must give the ultimate good that a creation can receive.

Since He alone is the embodiment of true good, His desire to do good can only be fulfilled by allowing another to partake in that very same inherent good, which is the complete and true good. However, this good is found only in Him. His wisdom, therefore, decreed that the realization of this bestowal should be through providing a space for creations to connect with Him, to the extent of their ability.

This means that although it is impossible for them to attain the same level of perfection as His, by connecting with Him, they can achieve a certain degree of that perfection. They can delight in that true goodness, to the extent that they are capable. Thus, the intention of God in creation is for it to delight in His goodness, to the extent possible.

Nevertheless, His wisdom has determined that for the good to be complete, the recipient of this delight must possess the good themselves. In other words, they must acquire this good on their own, not simply receive it by chance. This resembles, to a certain extent, His own perfection. For He, blessed be He, is inherently perfect, not by chance. Perfection is an intrinsic part of Him, and deficiencies are inherently absent from Him, because of the true nature of His being.

God's wisdom has decreed that for the good to be complete, the one delighting in it must take possession of that good themselves. This means that they must acquire the good through their own efforts, not just stumble upon it. This is a semblance of God's own inherent perfection, not a perfection that just happens to be there. For God is perfect by His very nature, without any deficiencies. His very essence demands perfection and excludes any flaws. However, nothing besides

God can possess this inherent nature. To somewhat resemble Him, a being must at least strive for perfection on their own, not have it imposed upon them, and eliminate any potential deficiencies.

Therefore, God has arranged for both perfection and deficiency to be possible outcomes. He created beings with the potential for both, providing them with the means to attain perfection and eradicate deficiencies on their own. In doing so, they resemble their Creator as closely as possible, making them worthy of connecting with Him and delighting in His goodness.

Furthermore, as these created beings strive for perfection and increasingly resemble their Creator, they also draw closer to Him. This process continues until achieving perfection and being in close connection with Him become one and the same. This is because His existence, blessed be He, is the epitome of true perfection. Therefore, any form of inherent perfection belongs solely to Him, like a branch originates from a root. Although the branch may not reach the original perfection of the root, it is nonetheless an extension and result of that initial perfection.

You can see that true perfection belongs only to His existence, and any deficiency is simply the concealment of His goodness and the hiding of His presence. The revelation of His presence and closeness to Him are the root causes of all perfection. Conversely, the hiding of His presence is the root cause of all deficiencies. The degree of His presence determines the level of perfection, and its absence results in deficiency.

Humanity stands balanced, influenced by the revelation or concealment of God's presence. By actively pursuing perfection and acquiring it through their own efforts, humans grab hold of Him, who is the source of all perfection. The more they perfect themselves, the stronger their connection and closeness to Him become. Eventually, the ultimate achievement of perfection and the ultimate closeness to Him become synonymous, resulting in delight in His goodness and true perfection.

For these dynamics of perfection and deficiency to exist, and for humanity to have the capacity for both as well as the ability to acquire one and remove the other – and for the means towards this perfection to be accessible – there must be a myriad of details in creation. These details are interrelated until the ultimate purpose is fully realized. However, the creation intended for this grand purpose of connection with God is deemed the primary creation. Everything else in existence serves to assist this primary creation in achieving its ultimate purpose.

Specifically, humans represent the true primary creation. All other creations, whether of a higher or lower order, exist solely to aid humanity in fulfilling its complete spiritual purpose in all its varied aspects and requirements. We will delve deeper into this topic later, God willing. For now, understand that wisdom and virtuous character traits are aspects of perfection, meant to refine humanity. Physicality and imagination, on the other hand, are aspects of deficiency, between which humans navigate to achieve their own state of perfection.

The Kabbalist and the Philosopher - Meamar Havikuach

Philosopher: Peace be upon you, my brother! How good is your coming at this time, for I am in great need of you.

Kabbalist: How can a philosopher need a kabbalist? You have already let your thoughts roam all corners of creation and subjugated it under you with your decisive proofs. How can I be of use to you?

Philosopher: Excessive praise is nothing but mockery. Let us come to the matter at hand. I will speak to you with the integrity of my heart, as is the way of our friendship. I have read and heard some matters from your Kabbalah, and they seem quite strange to me, for they contradict my investigations entirely. However, since I saw many pious individuals who followed its ways, I said to myself that I would see what you have to say. Perhaps I will hear from you something that, if not compelling, will at least not be contradictory and foolish according to sound reason, as it currently appears to me, leaving me no choice but to reject it.

Kabbalist: I will do as you say and inform you of the truth as it was transmitted to us by those who know the truth. The entire benefit of this knowledge will be that you receive from me another piece of knowledge: that you know that all a person can grasp through his philosophical inquiry is considered as nothing compared to what he can grasp through the true Kabbalah. Regarding this, the wise one said: "For the Lord gives wisdom, from His mouth come knowledge and understanding" (Proverbs 2:6). Now open your mouth wide, and I will fill it.

Philosopher: First, I wish to know from you about the sefirot that you mention - what are they? I would like to know this clearly, for I have heard such strange things about them that I had to restrain myself out of respect from crying out in the streets how astonished I was by them. I was nearly forced to say that they are nonsensical matters.

Kabbalist: Tell me what you heard about this.

Philosopher: I heard it said that they are one light that the Emanator, blessed be He, emanated from His primordial light, and that He, blessed be He, garbs Himself within them like a soul within a body.

Kabbalist: What else did you hear about this?

Philosopher: I heard that there is Atzilut, and there is Beriah, Yetzirah, and Asiyah. The difference between them is that Beriah, Yetzirah, and Asiyah are nothing but an illumination from this emanated light that we mentioned, and that it is divided into two parts. The inner part of it, meaning the soul, is called Divinity, while from the soul and below it is no longer called Divinity, but rather the "World of Separation." This applies to all three worlds.

Kabbalist: What do you say about this?

Philosopher: By the life of my soul, I do not even know how to arrange my difficulties due to their great quantity and quality, for this contradicts all reason and the truth of our faith.

Kabbalist: How so?

Four Difficulties Regarding the Sefirot of Atzilut

Philosopher: From now on, you will not escape one of these two options: Either you will say that they are Divinity, or not.

Kabbalist: But you already heard about this, that Atzilut is Divinity.

Philosopher: If it is Divinity, how can you conceive in your mind that Divinity can be derived from Divinity?

You said two things - that this contradicts all reason and our faith.

Philosopher: Indeed, regarding reason, it is as I said. For how can it be conceived that Divinity derives from Divinity? For God, meaning that Unique One who must exist to be the head of all creatures - since they are many, it is impossible for them to be conducted in an equal and fixed order except by a single head over them all. Therefore, we must understand that Unique One as the ultimate unity. How can we conceive of plurality, birth, and derivation of light within Him?

As for faith, tell me now, is this notion so far, God forbid, from the belief of the Christians, may their name be obliterated, who posited the Trinity, saying that He is three and He is one? For the One actually derives progeny from Himself, and yet it is all one. Furthermore, that which is renewed must not have existed prior to its renewal. If you say that the sefirot are new divinity, while the Infinite is ancient divinity, is this not exactly what is said about such things: "They chose new gods" (Judges 5:8)?

Additionally, how greatly do you stumble in faith, for we know that the Holy One, blessed be He, is absolutely simple, unaffected by any bodily contingencies. According to your words, there is no greater contingency than this - that His essence, blessed be He, should transform from non-existence to existence.

Kabbalist: You have already shaken the entire world with your words. Do you have any more such difficulties?
Philosopher: Indeed, I do. For now I spoke in general only about the matter of Atzilut. When we come to Beriah, Yetzirah, and Asiyah - they are exceedingly numerous. In truth, I have such strong questions and difficulties there that no mind of a wise and understanding person can bear them.

Kabbalist: Please state your words, and let me know what you have to say about this.

The Way to Spiritual Integrity

Difficulties Regarding the Sefirot of Beriah, Yetzirah, Asiyah

Philosopher: When you come to Beriah, Yetzirah, Asiyah, you make a continuum, and still call it Divinity. Afterward, you say that part of it is called Divinity, while part of it is not called by this name. Tell me, by your life, have you ever heard that Divinity could be divided to such an extent that half of it remains Divinity while half of it does not, but rather becomes a subservient slave to the first half? Believe me, faithful friend, these are not words of wisdom. It is impossible to bring such matters to the ears of an intelligent person, only to the simple-minded who believe everything.

However, there are two things I would like to know in any case: First, who involved us in this conflict? Second, what benefit emerges from this knowledge? Is the faith that the entire congregation of Israel believes - that the Creator is One, that He governs His world, that He gave His Torah to us, and that our Messiah will come - not good? What need do we have for all these matters of sefirot and worlds that breed nothing but confusion?

Kabbalist: Please complete your words.

Philosopher: I have one difficulty that encompasses all difficulties - that everything I have read or heard is astonishing from beginning to end. However, I think that if I would find at least one solid foundation upon which all these structures could be built, then perhaps the details would be comprehensible. But without that, why should I toil over the details when the entirety is difficult?

Can a Body Develop from Divinity?

However, I will not refrain from mentioning one strong difficulty I have with their words, which branches into two, but has one root:

I heard that you say that the sefirot developed level by level until this physical world came into being. This is an extremely difficult matter. What sense can there be to these words? How can that which is Divinity develop to the point of becoming one opaque body?

How Can We Understand the Emergence of the Other Side from Holiness?

The second, an even greater and more astounding difficulty, is what they say - that the Other Side emerged from the end of din (justice). Even more astonishing, they say that initially, good and evil were mixed together, and that is why the first worlds were destroyed, until the good was clarified by itself, which are the sefirot of holiness, and the evil by itself, which are the sefirot of the Other Side. To me, this matter seems almost like heresy, God forbid - to say that the Other Side was initially mixed into the sefirot, whether overtly or covertly. Say what you will, but they were one entity. How can one thing be clarified from it, with one part becoming the sefirot, which is Divinity, and the other part becoming the Other Side? I have no heart to accept these matters, and certainly not to utter them, for it seems to me that this leads to the heresy of two authorities, God forbid.

If the Sefirot are Divinity, How Can They Emanate from Divinity?

If you answer that the sefirot are light emanated from the Blessed Infinite One, and that is why such things are possible for them, this was already the first difficulty - how can one say that Divinity emanates from Divinity? If they are emanated from Him, they are outside of Him. Even if you say a hundred times that they are like a flame connected to a coal (Sefer Yetzirah 1:7), these are things said by mouth but are not accepted by the heart. For to say that something that is not essentially divine could still be divine is one of the impossibilities.

How Can We Understand Service Via the Sefirot?

Furthermore, according to your approach, all service is via the sefirot, and I see no permissibility for this. For we cannot escape the following: If they are not Divinity itself, then they must be able to be separate from Him and exist as vessels without light, like a body without a soul. Yet they are still described with the very attributes of Divinity - this is improper. For "the God of gods is the Lord" (Psalms 50:1), meaning the Holy One, blessed be He. According to your ways, it would mean Chesed, Gevurah, Tiferet. According to our faith, it is impossible to use these names for anyone other than the Emanator, blessed be He. Rather, "You shall have no other gods before Me" (Exodus 20:3).

If you answer that Divinity cleaves to them to such an extent that they are called by His name - such a thing should never be uttered, for you would be giving an opening to heretics, God forbid, and even worse.

In summary, these matters are very perplexing. Now, if you have the means to resolve them, if not entirely, then at least some of them, I would rejoice greatly.

Kabbalist: Until now, you have made yourself the witness, the judge, and the litigant. I, too, like you, will place you between Him and me as the adjudicator. Your reason will be the one I anticipate, as will you. But incline your ear and set aside your desire for just a moment, until you receive the true knowledge with a clear mind. Indeed, it requires resolution and conciliation.

Philosopher: Speak, and I shall listen.

Kabbalist: You are mistaken in every respect.

Philosopher: But I have heard many of your Kabbalists speak the very things I said.

Kabbalist: Their words need to be properly understood, not taken superficially.

Philosopher: Now let me hear a clear explanation from you.

The Way to Spiritual Integrity

This Wisdom Teaches the Unity of God and the Integrity of His Governance with Great Wisdom

Kabbalist: The foundation of this entire wisdom is the unity of the Emanator, blessed be He, that He is one in every way, without any change, plurality, or bodily contingency whatsoever.

Philosopher: The foundation is very good, if it can bear its structure.

Kabbalist: The entire matter of the wisdom of Kabbalah is nothing but an explanation of the attribute of His justice, blessed be He, the order of the laws of governance - how the Holy One, blessed be He, causes and governs all affairs of His world with great wisdom.

Philosopher: If this is what we would find in this wisdom, we would find something great. However, I do not see this wisdom proceeding along this path.

How Can We Understand Development in the Sefirot?

Kabbalist: Did I not tell you that you are mistaken in every respect?

Philosopher: I am stating what I gathered from the matters I read in your texts. I saw that you want to explain the chain of development - how the created being emerges from the Creator, as if the Creator, blessed be He, is the primary substance of the creations, developing from Him Himself. This primary substance gradually develops until it reaches the creations themselves. These are the sefirot and all that you expound upon regarding them. For you say that the Creator, blessed be He, placed His very name and was affected in one way until His own light was found to be affected and progressively developing until the lowest level was found. Now, if this matter could truly be stated, it would be very nice. For this development would certainly be the cause of all existences, and their variations would cause the variations in the world's affairs. Therefore, it would be good to know it, especially since the matter lends itself to attributing to it all the mitzvot and service, for it needs to be ordered according to its good nature. However, as I prefaced, if it could be said - for how can it be said that the light of the Creator, blessed be He, is affected or develops? You yourself have already admitted that contingencies do not apply to the Emanator, blessed be He.

Kabbalist: I acknowledge all this, and on the contrary, this is the foundation of my entire structure - that the Emanator, blessed be He, is not subject to any bodily contingency. But I said that you are mistaken in every respect, and I repeat it. It is impossible to say in any way that His light, blessed be He, is itself affected and develops to the extent that the Creator becomes a creation. Have you never heard that creation is something from nothing? If so, how can development and affectedness be spoken of?

Philosopher: Yes, your words have added water, now see to it that you add flour.

Understanding This Wisdom is Knowing His Governance, Blessed Be He

Kabbalist: But you will see that it is impossible for great sages to err in this, such as those from whom the Kabbalah flows to us. However, I will demonstrate to you that you did not understand anything of what you read. Do you know how to explain these levels mentioned in the sefirot, and all their variations mentioned at all times, what their benefit is in creation? How action and deed will result from them below? But inform me of the details, not generalities. If you know this, you can say that you understood what you read. If not, you will certainly say that you read what you did not understand.

Philosopher: Yes, in general I tell you that they are all matters needed to bring about the development of the world, and that through their differences in their states, they differentiate the affairs of the world. But in particular, I do not know what they are - not the qav (line) or the reshimu (impression), not Adam Kadmon, nor his worlds, the tikunim (rectifications) of the partzufim (visages) and their garments and intervals - all these are numerous. These are things I have read but do not know their nature. I only see great difficulties in them.

Kabbalist: If so, you do not know. I will start you on one path so you may see what you had not considered in these matters.

Philosopher: Speak.

Infinite and Sefirot - What He Can Will and What He Willed

Kabbalist: The Emanator, blessed be He, is certainly the Master of will, according to what He willed and wills. Now we can speak of Him in two aspects: in terms of His essence and in terms of His will. Do you admit this or not?

Philosopher: Certainly, we can speak about any subject in terms of each aspect of it independently. For example, when speaking about a person's affairs, the person is called the subject of the discussions, meaning the qualities being discussed about him are called the aspect or aspects of him. We can discuss an aspect of the person - that he is learned, charitable, or wise. Each of these is an independent aspect that we can discuss regarding each subject on its own.

Kabbalist: Regarding the essence of the Emanator, blessed be He, we are forbidden to speak of it, and we do not even need to delve into it at all. For it suffices us to know of His existence. When we know that He is the ultimate perfection, that He is omnipotent - we know what we need to know in this matter. Beyond this, we are already forbidden to even speak. Therefore, we will no longer speak of His essence, only of His will, for this is closer to us and is permissible, as we are not touching upon His essence at all.

Philosopher: It is good to speak of His will. But what can you say? His will has no end, His thought has no limit. What can you investigate regarding that which has no bounds or finitude?

Kabbalist: This is precisely what I wanted to elicit from you, that you admit that there is no end to His will and thought. From now on, you will not be able to flee from me concerning what I wish to impart to you. Please tell me, you certainly believe in reward and punishment, for it is one of the fundamentals of faith. But tell me: There are deeds in the world for which the Holy One, blessed be He, desires to benefit their doers, and there are those for which He desires to punish.

There is a time when He elevates and a time when He lowers; a time when He impoverishes and a time when He enriches. If so, in His will there is certainly a will of beneficence, a will of harm, a will of lowering, and a will of elevating. All this is certainly in order, for there is an order to the governance. If so, we can certainly discuss all of this, as we are not touching upon His essence, blessed be He, at all. In summary, these are the attributes of His will that we can certainly investigate and know.

www.ingramcontent.com/pod-product-compliance
Lightning Source LLC
LaVergne TN
LVHW091358210726
843527LV00001B/45